Power From On High

The Two Hundredth Anniversary of the Great Moravian Revival 1727-1927

CTM Prayer Classics

Common Thread Ministries has published a number of out of print and no longer under copyright works for your enjoyment. These books are available on our website.

- **Power From On High**
  - The Two Hundredth Anniversary of the Great Moravian Revival 1727-1927 with Study Questions
- **A Threefold Cord**
  - Daily Devotional Readings from the 1830's
- **Rainbows of Promises — Book 1**
  - A Children's Book of New Testament Verses from 1887
- **Rainbows of Promises — Book 2**
  - A Children's Book of Old Testament Verses from 1887

Power From On High

The Two Hundredth Anniversary of the
Great Moravian Revival 1727-1927

Original by: John Greenfield

2017 Edition By: Mark Mirza

CTM Prayer Classics
CTM Publishing Inc.
2017

First Printing: 2017

Trade Paperback: ISBN 978-0-9972365-5-2
Kindle: ISBN 978-0-9972365-6-9
ePub: ISBN 978-0-99723656-7-6

CTM Publishing, Inc.
850 Piedmont Ave NE, Suite # 1506
Atlanta, GA 30308

wwwMarkMirza.com

Ordering Information:

Special discounts are available on quantity purchases by corporations, associations, educators, and others. For details, contact the publisher at the above listed address.

U.S. trade bookstores and wholesalers: Please contact CTM Publishing, Inc. Tel: (404) 606-2322; or email Mark@CTMPrayer.org

Dedication

To the Lord's church that he has allowed me to serve as a fellow bondsman.

Thank you.

Thank you for the opportunity to share insights about the Power From On High that we have access to through our prayers.

And I continue to pray Paul's words to the church at Colossae over you:

Continue earnestly in prayer,
being vigilant in it with thanksgiving;
meanwhile praying also for us,
that God would open to us a door for the word,
to speak the mystery of Christ...
that I may make it manifest,
as I ought to speak.
(Colossians 4:2-4)

Contents

ABOUT THIS CTM PRAYER CLASSIC   **10**

FOREWORD   **11**

INTRODUCTION   **15**

CHAPTER 1 - A MODERN PENTECOST   **19**

Pentecost may be repeated. Testimony of D. L. Moody and Moravian historians. Striking similarity of the Jerusalem and Herrnhut Pentecosts.

CHAPTER 2 - WHEN THE SPIRIT CAME   **31**

Prayer always precedes Pentecost. Count Zinzendorf preeminently a man of prayer. Days and nights of praying in Herrnhut. Organization of Society of Hourly Intercession.

CHAPTER 3 - THE SPIRIT'S WITNESS   **45**

The witness of the Spirit to the believer of his pardon, justification and adoption. A little girl's conversion and her joyful assurance of salvation. John Wesley's Conversion.

CHAPTER 4 - WITNESS UNTO ME   **59**

The Holy Spirit always glorifies Christ. Moravian theology becomes pre-eminently Christology. His Deity and His Death the great theme of their songs and sermons. Dr. Thomas Chalmers' Testimony.

CHAPTER 5 - A NEW SONG   **73**

Great hymns are born in revivals. Baptism with the Holy Spirit filled Herrnhut Moravians with spiritual songs. German and English Moravian Hymn writers. Calvary and Pentecost their constant theme.

CHAPTER 6 - FRUIT THAT ABIDES   **85**

August 13, 1727, was but the beginning of the great revival. Year after year it grew in volume and force. Herrnhut became a spiritual Mecca. Evangelism, Foreign Missions, Hymnology and Schools are some of the abiding fruit.

CHAPTER 7 - RENEW OUR DAYS   **97**

Prayer of Jeremiah becomes the prayer of great Moravian Bishop John Amos Comenius, and of restorer of Brethrens' Church, Count Zinzendorf. Prayer for renewal of those great spiritual experiences our greatest need to-day. Charlee Wesley's Conversion. The Baptism with the Holy Spirit.

About This CTM Prayer Classic

In this book, we have added a study guide to go with a classic history of the Moravian Revival and Prayer movement.

The movement began in 1727 and this history, written by the Reverend John Greenfield, a Moravian Evangelist, was published in 1928 for the two hundredth anniversary of the great Moravian Revival.

We have also included a foreword written by David Butts, the President of Harvest Prayer Ministries.

As you read this, let the Holy Spirit prompt your heart to:

1) Renew your views on revival (Luke 24:49)
2) Review your assurance of your salvation (Romans 8:16)
3) Reflect on your life as one called unto good works (Ephesians 2:10)

The same wording styles and punctuation have been retained as they were used in the original printing, including the absence of periods in many locations — and we let that style remain.

We have though, cleaned up a particular printing issue, consistent with older printers, regarding punctuation marks. Many of them sit a space beyond where they should be. For example, "faith ;" has been changed to "faith;" and so on.

Foreword

History is filled with stories of the moves of the Spirit of God that stir our souls and encourage our faith. One of the most exciting and practical for us today is the account of the Moravians of Herrnhut who experienced a powerful revival in 1727 that continues to impact the world in our day. Many would trace the beginnings of the modern missions' movement to the revival among the Moravians and their radical obedience in following Christ to the ends of the earth.

My friend, Mark Mirza, has provided a great service to the Body of Christ by taking an account of this revival, written 200 years after it began, by John Greenfield, and making it available in a most usable form. Mark's study questions at the end of each chapter allows this to be a tool for small groups and individuals that can be used to stir much prayer for revival. The addition of the study questions, moves this from simply being an historical account to a personal challenge for revival.

Many are writing on revival with the hope of seeing such a move of God in our day. *Power From On High*, grounds that hope in history and at the same time provides the practical help for a movement of prayer that prepares the way for the Spirit to do His work in the Church today.

David Butts

President, Harvest Prayer Ministries
www.HarvestPrayer.com

POWER FROM ON HIGH
OR
THE TWO HUNDREDTH ANNIVERSARY
OF
OF THE GREAT MORAVIAN REVIVAL
1727-1927

REV. JOHN GREENFIELD
Moravian Evangelist

To overt from men God's wrath
Jesus suffered in our stead;
By an ignominious death
He a full atonement made;
And by His most precious blood
Bought us, sinners, nigh to God.

But examine first your case,
Whether you be in the faith;
Do you long for pardoning grace?
Is your only hope His death?
Then, howe'er your soul's opprest,
Come, you are a worthy guest.

Composed by John Huss, circa 1400,
several years before his martyrdom.
Oldest Moravian Hymn known.

This work was originally Published by

The World Wide Revival Prayer Movement
5, South Oxford Place, Ventnor
Atlantic City, N.J.

MARSHALL, MORGAN & SCOTT, LTD.
Office of the Life of Faith
1, 2, 11, 12, Paternoster Buildings, London, E.C.4
And 99, George Street, Edinburgh

Based on the World-Wide Revival Prayer
Movement Edition

Originally Made and printed in Great Britain
by
Hunt, Barnard & Co., Ltd.
London & Aylesbury

Introduction

"He shall baptize you with the Holy Ghost and with fire" (Matthew iii. 11).

"And He said unto them. These are the words which I spake unto you, while was yet with you, that all things must be fulfilled, which were written in the law of Moses, and in the prophets and in the Psalms concerning Me! Then opened He their understanding that they might understand the Scriptures. And He said unto them, Thus it is written, and thus it behoved Christ to suffer, and to rise from the dead the third: and that repentance and remission of sin should be preached in His Name among all nations, beginning at Jerusalem. And ye are witnesses of these things. And, behold, I send the promise of My Father upon you: but tarry ye in the city of Jerusalem, until ye be endued with power from on high" (Luke xxiv. 44—49).

"And, being assembled together with them, He commanded them that they should not depart from Jerusalem, but wait for the promise of the Father, which, saith He, you have heard of Me. For John truly baptized with water; but ye shall be baptized with the Holy Ghost not many days hence. When they therefore come together, they asked of Him saying, Lord, wilt Thou at this time restore again the kingdom to Israel? And He said unto them, It is not for you to know the times or the seasons, which the Father hath put in His own power. But ye shall receive power, after that the Holy Ghost is come upon you: and ye shall be witnesses unto Me both in Jerusalem, and in all Judea, and in Samaria, and unto the uttermost part of the earth" (Acts i. 4—8).

"And when the day of Pentecost was fully come, they were all with one accord in one place. And suddenly there came a sound from heaven as of a rushing mighty wind, and it filled all the house where they were sitting. And there appeared unto them cloven tongues like as of fire, and it sat upon each of them. And they were all filled with the Holy Ghost, and began to speak with other tongues, the Spirit gave them utterance" (Acts ii. 1-4).

"And when they had prayed, the place was shaken where they were assembled together; and they were all filled with Holy Ghost, and they spake the Word of God, with boldness" (Acts iv. 31).

"And they chose Stephen, a man full of faith and of the Holy Ghost" (Acts vi. 5).

"Now when the Apostles which were at Jerusalem heard that Samaria had received the Word of God, they sent unto them Peter and John: who, when they were come down, prayed for them, that they might receive the Holy Ghost: (For as yet He was fallen upon none of them: only they were baptized in the Name of the Lord Jesus.) Then laid they their hands on them, and they received the Holy Ghost" (Acts viii. 14—17).

"While Peter yet spake these words, the Holy Ghost fell on all them which heard the Word. And they of the circumcision which believed were astonished, as many as came with Peter, because that on the Gentiles also was poured out the gift of the Holy Ghost" (Acts x. 44-45).

JOHN GREENFIELD

POWER FROM ON HIGH

"The baptism in the Holy Ghost was given once for all on the day of Pentecost, when the Paraclete came in person to make His abode in the Church. It does not follow therefore that every believer has received this baptism. God's gift is one thing; our appropriation of that gift is quite another thing. Our relation to the second and to the third persons of the Godhead is exactly parallel in this respect. 'God so loved the world that He gave His only begotten Son.' (John 3:16.) 'But as many as received Him to them gave He the right to become the children of God, even to them that believe on His name.' (John 1:12.) Here are the two sides of salvation, the divine and the human, which are absolutely co-essential.' It seems clear from the Scriptures that it is still the duty and privilege of believers to receive the Holy Spirit by a conscious, definite act of appropriating faith, just as they received Jesus Christ."

— *The Ministry of the Spirit*, A. J. Gordon, D. D.

"It seems to me beyond question, as a matter of experience both of Christians in the present day and of the early Church, as recorded by inspiration, that in addition to the gift of the Spirit received at conversion, there is another blessing corresponding in its signs and effects to the blessing received by the Apostles at Pentecost- blessing to be asked for and expected by Christians still, and to be described in language similar to that employed in the Book of Acts. Whatever that blessing may be, it is in immediate connection with the Holy Ghost.... It is only when He is consciously accepted in all His power that we can be said to be either 'baptized' or 'filled' with the Holy Ghost."

— *Through the Eternal Spirit,* James Elder Cumming

Chapter 1

A MODERN PENTECOST

Lord God, the Holy Ghost,
In this accepted hour,
As on the day of Pentecost,
Descend in all Thy Power.

We meet with one accord,
in our appointed place,
And wait the promise of our Lord,
The Spirit of all grace.

The young, the old inspire,
With wisdom from above;
And give us hearts and tongues of fire,
To pray, and praise, and love.

THUS sang the Scotch Moravian poet and hymnwriter, James Montgomery, more than a hundred years ago. His prayer for another Pentecost was undoubtedly inspired by the experiences of his spiritual fathers on August 13, 1727, in Herrnhut, Germany. We are now celebrating the Bi-Centennial of what our Moravian Text Book calls the "Signal outpouring of the Holy Spirit experienced by the congregation of Herrnhut." We do well to join in Montgomery's earnest prayer for another Pentecost in our own day. D. L. Moody in one of his last sermons in Boston, his spiritual birthplace, spoke thus of the Holy Spirit:

"See how He came on the day of Pentecost! It is not carnal to pray that He come again and that the place may be shaken. I believe Pentecost was but a specimen day. I think the Church has made this woeful mistake that Pentecost was a miracle never to be repeated. I have thought too that Pentecost was a miracle that is not to be repeated. I believe now if we looked on Pentecost as a specimen day and began to pray, we should have the old Pentecostal fire here in Boston."

A Moravian historian writes in a similar vein as follows: "God says: 'It shall come to pass-I will pour.' This was His promise through the prophet Joel. The first fulfillment of this promise was on the day of Pentecost. There is nothing in the New Testament to indicate that this was to be the one and only fulfillment of this promise. On the contrary we read in the book of Acts of many outpourings of the Holy Spirit, as in Samaria (8:14-17) as in Ephesus (19:1-7) and even in the case of the Gentiles (10:44-46). Church History also abounds in records of special outpourings of the Holy Ghost, and verily the thirteenth of August 1727 was a day of the outpouring of the Holy Spirit. We saw the hand of God and His wonders, and we were all under the cloud of our fathers baptized with their Spirit. The Holy Ghost came upon us and in those days great signs and wonders took place in our midst. From that time scarcely a day passed but what we beheld His almighty workings amongst us. A great hunger after the Word of God took possession of us so that we had to have three services every day, viz., 5:00 and 7:30 A. M. and 9:00 P. M. Everyone desired above everything else that the Holy Spirit might have full control. Self-love and self-will as well as all disobedience disappeared and an overwhelming flood of grace swept us all out into the great ocean of Divine Love."

Exactly what happened that Wednesday forenoon, August 13th, 1727, in the specially called Communion service at Berthelsdorf, none of the participants could fully describe. They left the house of God that noon "hardly knowing whether they belonged to earth or had already gone to Heaven." Count Zinzendorf gave the following account of it a number of years afterwards to a British audience.

"We needed to come to the communion with a sense of the loving nearness of the Savior. This was the great comfort which has made this day a generation ago to be a festival, because on this day twenty-seven years ago the Congregation of Herrnhut, assembled for communion (at the Berthelsdorf church), were all dissatisfied with themselves. They had quit judging each other because they had become convinced, each one, of his lack of worth in the sight of God and each felt himself at this communion to be in view of the noble countenance of the Savior.

O head so full of bruises,
So full of pain and scorn.

"In this view of the man of sorrows and acquainted with grief, their hearts told them that He would be their patron and their priest, who was at once changing their tears into oil of gladness, and their misery into happiness. This firm confidence changed them in a single moment into a happy people which they are to this day and into their happiness they have since led many thousands of others through the memory and the help which the heavenly grace once given to themselves, so many thousand times confirmed to them since then."

The following summary is by our beloved Bishop Edward Rondthaler:

"Zinzendorf, who gives us the deepest and most vivid account of this wonderful occurence, says it was 'a sense of the nearness of Christ' bestowed in a single moment, upon all the members that were present; and it was so unanimous that two members, at work twenty miles away, unaware that the meeting was being held, became at the same time deeply conscious of the same blessing."

"These members were all laity, though at a later time, ministers and missionaries, deacons, presbyters and bishops arose out of the wonderfully blessed assemblage. They were all lay people, in the experience of Christ which they made, and yet in another sense they were all ministers of Christ,-'A holy priesthood, to offer up spiritual sacrifices, acceptable to God by Jesus Christ.'-I. Peter 2:5."

"It was a young congregation which received the 13th of August blessing. Zinzendorf, the human leader, was just twenty-seven years old, and if a census had been taken, it would have been found that his own age was approximately the average of the whole company. Throughout the story of the early labors of the Renewed Church we are impressed with the comparative youth of the men and women who made such wonderful ventures of faith for Jesus Christ."

Verily the history of the Moravian Church confirms the doctrine of the great American Evangelist as to the need and possibility of the baptism with the Holy Ghost. The spiritual experiences of the Moravian Brethren two centuries ago bear a striking resemblance to the Pentecostal power and results in the days of the Apostles. The company of believers both at Jerusalem and Herrnhut numbered less than three hundred souls. Both congregations were humanly speaking totally devoid of worldly influence, wisdom, power and wealth. Their enemies called them "unlearned and ignorant." Their best friend described them in the following language: "Ye see your calling, brethren, how that not many wise men after the flesh, not many mighty, not many noble are called; but God hath chosen the foolish things of the world to confound the wise, and God hath chosen the weak things of the world to confound the things which are mighty; and the base things of the world, and things which are despised, hath God chosen, yea, and things which are not, to bring to naught things that are, that no flesh should glory in His presence." I. Cor. 1:26-28.

On both these small and weak congregations God poured out His Holy Spirit and endued them with power from on high. At once these believers, naturally timid and fearful, were transformed into flaming evangelists. Supernatural knowledge and power seemed to possess them. "Mouth and wisdom" were given them which "none of their adversaries were able to gainsay or resist." Opposition and persecution scattered the Jerusalem congregation but could not silence their testimony, for we are told: "Therefore, they that were scattered abroad went everywhere preaching the Word." Acts 8:4. Similar experiences were the lot of the Moravian Brethren. Sprung from the labors and martyr-death of the great Bohemian Reformer, John Huss, "the Brethren" had passed through centuries of persecution. Many had sealed their testimony with their blood. imprisonment, torture and banishment had caused them to forsake the homes of their fathers and flee for refuge to Germany where a young Christian nobleman, Count Zinzendorf, offered them an asylum on his estates in Saxony. They named their new home Herrnhut, "the Lord's Watch," and from this place after their baptism with the Holy Spirit, they became the world's evangelists and missionaries. Their new leader, Count Zinzendorf, could truly sing of them:

Everywhere with shoutings loud,
Shouts that shake the gates of Hell,
Thy anointed witness-cloud
Of Thy great Redemption tell.

Of the Apostolic Church at Jerusalem a certain writer has said: "Before thirty years had elapsed from the death of Christ, His followers had spread from Palestine throughout Syria; through almost all the numerous districts of Asia Minor; through Greece and the Islands of the Aegean Sea, the coast of Africa, and even into Italy and Rome." And at the close of the first century Justin Martyr could truly testify: "There is not a nation either Greek or Barbarian or of any other name, even those who wander in tribes or live in tents, among whom prayers and thanksgiving are not offered to the Father and Creator of the Universe in the name of the Crucified Jesus."

Similar testimony may be borne to the labors of the Moravian Brethren. During the first three decades after their spiritual Pentecost they carried the Gospel of salvation by the blood of the Lamb not only to nearly every country in Europe but also to many pagan races in America, North and South, Asia and Africa. Their first mission was to the Negroes in the West Indies, five years after the out-pouring of the Spirit. The following year they sent out missionaries to Greenland, which Cowper has immortalized in the well-known lines on Hope:

> See Germany send forth
> Her sons to pour it on the farthest North;
> Fired with a zeal peculiar they defy
> The rage and rigor of a polar sky,
> And plant successfully sweet Sharon's Rose
> On icy plains and in eternal snows.

Fifty years before the beginning of modern Foreign Missions by William Carey, the Moravian Church had led the way into pagan countries both by precept and example. Their English Missionary Magazine, "Periodical Accounts," inspired Dr. Carey and in a meeting of his Baptist brethren he threw a copy of the paper on a table with these memorable and historic words:

"See what the Moravians have done! Cannot we follow their example and in obedience to our Heavenly Master go out into the world, and preach the Gospel to the heathen?"

So generally has the leadership of the Moravian Church in Foreign Missions been recognized that the well-known German historian of "Protestant Missions," Dr. Warneck, testifies:

"This small Church in twenty years called into being more Missions than the whole Evangelical Church has done in two centuries."

A hundred years pass by since that marvelous baptism with the Holy Spirit-years of almost continuous revival and blessed missionary service. So numerous are their missionary stations that it may truly be said the sun never sets on them. Dr. Thomas Chalmers, Scotland's greatest preacher and leader, bears this eloquent testimony to Moravian Missionaries:

"It is now a century since they have had intercourse with men in the infancy of civilization. During that time they have been laboring in all the different quarters of the world, and have succeeded in reclaiming many a wild region to Christianity. One of their principles in carrying on the business of missions, is, not to interfere with other men's labors; and thus it is that one so often meets with them among the outskirts of the species, making glad some solitary place, and raising a sweet vineyard in some remote and unfrequented wilderness. Oh, when one looks at the number and greatness of their achievements, when he thinks of the change they have made on materials so coarse and unpromising; when he eyes the villages they have formed and he witnesses the love and listens to the piety of reclaimed savages-who would not long to be in possession of the charm by which they have wrought this wondrous transformation? Who would not willingly exchange for it all the parade of human eloquence and all the confidence of human argument?"

We have entitled this chapter, "A Modern Pentecost" and would close it with the words of the sainted Moravian Bishop, Evelyn Hasse:

"Just as the Infant Church in Jerusalem in apostolic days had its Pentecost, from which its members went forth to be Christ's witnesses 'both in Jerusalem and in all Judea and in Samaria, and unto the uttermost parts of the earth,' so had this church also its own experiences of the quickening power of the Holy Ghost, when in 1727 He came upon its members gathered at the table of the Lord, and baptized them all into one body, and filled them with a strong, unquenchable passion to execute the Saviour's great Commission, and to let all mankind know of His Cross and of His salvation."

> Urged by love, to every nation
> Of the fallen human race
> We will publish Christ's salvation,

And declare His blood-bought grace;
To display Him, and portray Him,
In His dying form and beauty,
Be our aim and joyful duty."

— Zinzendorf.

Such then was the thirteenth of August seventeen hundred and twenty-seven. Count Zinzendorf, the one outstanding human leader and spokesman, called it "the day of the outpouring of the Holy Spirit upon the congregation," - "its Pentecost." Again he described it as follows: "The Saviour permitted to come upon us a Spirit of whom we had hitherto not had any experience or knowledge." "Hitherto WE had been the leaders and helpers. Now the Holy Spirit Himself took full control of everything and everybody."

Therefore also he prayed to Jesus:

Lord, our High-Priest and Saviour,
Pour fire and Spirit's fervour
On all our priestly bands;
When we are interceding
And for Thy people pleading,
Give incense, and hold up our hands.

Questions for Chapter 1

QUESTION 1:

D. L. Moody said that he used to look at the Day of Pentecost as "...a miracle that is not to be repeated." Go back and reread Luke's record in Acts 2.

While the miracle referred to is described in Acts 2:1-4, we highly recommend reading all of chapter 1 and chapter 2. And then decide for yourself, is this a miracle that is not to be repeated, or is this "...a specimen day?" [NOTE: *By "a specimen day" Moody meant, "A day that is an example of what we can expect or experience."*]

QUESTION 2:

How do the outpourings of the Holy Spirit in Acts 8:14-17 (in Samaria), Acts 10:44-46 (upon Gentiles), and Acts 19:1-7 (in Ephesus) compare, and differ from the miracle recorded in chapter 2?

QUESTION 3:

Count Zinzendorf, himself a participant and witness to the August 13, 1727 Communion service at Bertheldorf Church described the spiritual state of the congregation as being "all dissatisfied with themselves. They had quit judging each other because they had become convinced, each one, of his lack of worth in the sight of God and each felt himself at this Communion to be in view of the noble countenance of the Saviour."

First, what did Zinzendorf mean?

Have you ever been in Communion with men and women who have this kind of a spirit?

QUESTION 4:

What was it that changed these folks' countenance?

Answer: It was "a sense of the _____ of Christ."

QUESTION 5:

What spiritual sacrifices are you offering up (1 Peter 2:5)? And are they acceptable to God?

QUESTION 6:

The Moravians faced physical and emotional persecution. What persecution have you faced?

QUESTION 7:

Like the first century church, the first 30 years of the Moravians accomplished much, what have you accomplished that glorifies God?

Are there things God has told you to do yet you have not?

What about your spiritual gifts, or motivational gifts, can you share with others what they are?

QUESTION 8:

What is meant by the words, "The Moravian Church had led the way into pagan countries both by precept and example?"

QUESTION 9:

Does God's precept or principle to share the gospel include you too?

QUESTION 10:

The Moravian Church's experience of "the quickening power of the Holy Ghost" in 1727 "filled them with a strong, unquenchable passion to execute the Saviour's great commission..."

What is your passion?

"As I went in and shut the door after me, it seemed as if I met the Lord Jesus Christ face to face.... He said nothing, but looked at me in such a manner as to break me right down at His feet. I wept aloud like a child, and made such confessions as I could with my choked utterance." ... "As I turned and was about to take a seat by the fire, I received a mighty baptism of the Holy Ghost.... No words can express the wonderful love that was shed abroad in my heart. I wept with joy and love."

— *Autobiography*, Charles G. Finney

"Every step of progress in the Christian life is taken by a fresh and fuller appropriation of Christ by faith, a fuller baptism of the Holy Spirit..... "As we are more and more emptied of all self-dependence, and as by faith we secure deeper and deeper baptisms of the Holy Ghost, and put on the Lord Jesus Christ more thoroughly, by just so much faster do we grow in the favor of God.... You must pray in faith for the Holy Spirit. At every forward step in your progress you must have a fresh anointing of the Holy Spirit through faith."

— *Lectures on Revivals*, Charles G. Finney

"Dr. George W. Gale had failed to receive that divine anointing of the Holy Ghost that would make him a power in the pulpit and in society for the conversion of souls. He had fallen short of receiving the baptism of the Holy Ghost, which is indispensable to ministerial success. When Christ commissioned His Apostles to go and preach He told them to abide at Jerusalem till they were endued with power from on high. This power was the baptism of the Holy Ghost poured out upon them on the day of Pentecost.... This is an indispensable qualification for success in the ministry and I have often been surprised and pained that to this day so little stress is laid upon this qualification for preaching Christ to a sinful world."

— *Autobiography*, Charles G. Finney

Chapter 2

WHEN THE SPIRIT CAME

PRAYER always precedes Pentecost. The Book of Acts describes many outpourings of The Holy Spirit, but never apart from prayer. In our own day the great Welsh and Korean revivals were preceded by months, if not years, of importunate and united praying. Hence the supreme importance of the prayer meeting, for it is "the power-house of the church." So our Fathers found it two centuries ago. The first part of the year 1727 did not seem very promising. Differences of opinion and heated controversy on doctrinal questions threatened to disrupt the congregation. The majority were members of the Ancient Moravian Church of the Brethren. But other believers had also been attracted to Herrnhut. Lutherans, Reformed, Baptists, etc., had joined the community. Questions of predestination, holiness, the meaning and mode of baptism, etc., etc., seemed likely to divide the believers into a number of small and belligerent sects. Then the more earnest and spiritual souls among them began to cry mightily unto the Lord for deliverance. His first answer was a general outpouring upon them of "the spirit of grace and supplications." (Zech. 12:10.) Matthew Henry's comment on this passage was fulfilled in their case:

"When God intends great mercy for His people, the first thing He does is to set them a praying."

He also sent them a human leader and deliverer in the person of the young German nobleman, Count Zinzendorf, who so kindly had offered this persecuted Church a place of refuge on his own estates. This godly youth and preeminent genius had been divinely prepared for his great work of spiritual leadership. Converted in early childhood he composed and signed at four years of age the following covenant: "Dear Saviour, do Thou be mine, and I will be Thine." He had chosen as his life-motto the now famous confession: "I have one passion: it is Jesus, Jesus only." Of his days and years at school he bears the following testimony: "I was not only preserved from committing gross sins, but in some instances succeeded in inducing those very persons, who had tried to mislead me, to join me in prayer; and thus I won some of them to Christ. This was not only the case at school but also in the

Universities which I attended, and on my travels ever since. Whilst at the Universities I exercised myself in physical accomplishments, because I deemed them useful; but 1 never indulged in dancing in promiscuous assemblies of both sexes, because I considered it wrong and sinful. I was as fond of amusements as any one; but as soon as an inordinate affection for them arose in my soul, I felt condemned. My whole soul continually tended to the Cross. I spoke with everyone I met on this subject."

Having finished the University courses his education was to be furthered by travel and a visit to foreign countries. But everywhere his master-passion of love for and fellowship with the Crucified Redeemer controlled him. In the Duesseldorf Gallery of paintings his attention was drawn with marked effect to a wonderfully expressive Ecce Homo, over which were the words:

Hoc feci pro te:
Quid facts pro me?

This have I done for thee;
What doest thou for Me

To a friend the young count wrote: "If the object of my being sent to France is to make me a man of the world, I declare that this is money thrown away; for God will in His goodness preserve in me the desire to live only for Jesus Christ." In Paris a Duchess asked him: "Good evening, Count; were you at the opera last night?" "No, Madame," he replied, "I have no time for the opera." "Oh, brilliant wretchedness!" he exclaimed on leaving this city. Such was the young nobleman whom the Lord sent to be the spiritual and temporal leader of several hundred earnest but quarrelling Christian refugees.

So effective and fruitful was this leadership that nearly two centuries later Professor Binnie of Scotland declared: "It would not be going too far to affirm that Count Zinzendorf did more than any other man to redeem the Eighteenth Century from the reproach of barrenness, in relation to evangelical teaching and work."

If we inquire as to the secret of his success, two Scripture texts suggest themselves, viz.: "Not by might, nor by power, but by my Spirit saith the Lord of Hosts." (Zech. 4:6.) "And when they had prayed, the place was shaken where they were assembled together, and they were all filled with the Holy Ghost, and they spake the word of God with boldness." (Acts 4:31.) Count Zinzendorf had early learned the secret of prevailing prayer. So active had he been in establishing circles for prayer, that on leaving the college at Halle, at sixteen years of age, he handed the famous Professor Francke a list of seven praying societies. Would that he might have many followers among the student body of today! How quickly this would solve all youthful as well as mature problems. It was a condition and not a theory which confronted the young nobleman in 1727 at Herrnhut. How to unite in faith and love and service the pious but disputatious followers of Huss, Luther, Calvin, Zwingle, Schwenkfeld, etc., etc., seemed indeed a hopeless problem apart from divine intervention. In answer to earnest and persevering prayer, superhuman wisdom guided the young Count in the use of certain means which proved of incalculable value. Bishop J. T. Hamilton has called attention to this in a recent article in The Moravian. After describing the Brotherly Covenant drawn up by Zinzendorf, calling upon them "to seek out and emphasize the points in which they agreed" rather than to stress their differences, and the Count's personal interview with every individual adult resident in Herrnhut, Bishop Hamilton says:

"But far more important than this was their entering into solemn covenant with Zinzendorf, that twelfth of May, to actually dedicate their lives, as he dedicated his, to the service of the Lord Jesus Christ, each one in his particular calling and position. This covenant was in essentials what constitutes our Brotherly Agreement of today, the link uniting our individual members and our corporate congregations with each other.

"There followed the choice of the twelve elders to complete the organization of the spiritual life of Herrnhut, and the appointment of persons to the various offices foreseen in the statutes. So order, itself a product of greater mutual confidence as well as of mutually recognized devotion, made possible provision for the Bible study and the frequent gathering of bands for prayer, that next marked the ensuing summer months and led the way to and prepared for the baptism of the Spirit that culminated on that blessed thirteenth of August, an enduement with power, that enabled those men and women of Herrnhut to serve their generation so effectively in evangelizing throughout Christendom and in heathendom and in keeping faith aglow during decades of rather general indifference and rationalism as well as in promoting an education that sought to cultivate the heart as well as to inform the intellect and to secure purity of morals."

Truly the great Moravian revival of 1727, which reached its climax August 13, was preceded and followed by most extraordinary praying. The spirit of grace and supplications manifested itself in the early part of the year. Count Zinzendorf began to give spiritual instructions to a class of nine girls between the ages of ten and thirteen years. "The Count," so the historian of that period tells us, "frequently complained to his consort that though the children behaved with great outward propriety, he could not perceive any traces of spiritual life among them; and however much might be said to them of the Lord Jesus Christ, yet it did not seem to reach their hearts. In this distress of his mind he took his refuge to the Lord in prayer, most fervently entreating Him to grant to these children His grace and blessing."

What a spectacle! A gifted, wealthy, young German nobleman on his knees, agonizing in prayer for the conversion of some little school girls! Later on we read as follows:

"July 16. The Count poured forth his soul in a heart-affecting prayer, accompanied with a flood of tears; this prayer produced an extraordinary effect, and was the beginning of the subsequent operation of the life-giving and energetic Spirit of God." Not only Count Zinzendorf, but many other brethren also began to pray as never before. In the "Memorial Days of the Renewed Moravian Church," we read as follows:

"July 22.-A number of Brethren, covenanted together of their own accord, engaging to meet often on the Hutberg, to pour out their hearts in prayer and hymns.

"On the fifth of August the Warden, viz., the Count, spent the whole night in watching, in company of about twelve or fourteen brethren. At midnight there was held on the Hutberg a large meeting for the purpose of prayer, at which great emotion prevailed.

"On Sunday, August 10, about noon, while Pastor Rothe was holding the meeting at Herrnhut, he felt himself overwhelmed by a wonderful and irresistible power of the Lord, and sunk down into the dust before God, and with him sunk down the whole assembled congregation, in an ecstasy of feeling. In this frame of mind they continued till midnight engaged in prayer and singing, weeping and supplication.

"After that distinguished day of blessing, the 13th of August, 1727, on which the Spirit of grace and supplication had been poured out upon the congregation at Herrnhut, the thought struck some brethren and sisters that it might be well to set apart certain hours for the purpose of prayer, at which seasons all might be reminded of its excellency, and be induced by the promise annexed to fervent prayer to pour out their hearts before the Lord.

"It was moreover considered as an important point that, as in the days of the Old Covenant, the sacred fire was never permitted to go out on the altar (Lev. 6:13 and 14), so in a congregation which is a temple of the living God, wherein He has His altar and His fire, the intercession of His saints should incessantly rise up unto Him like holy incense.

"On August 26 twenty-four brethren and the same number of sisters met, and covenanted together to continue from one midnight to the next in prayer, dividing for that purpose the twenty-four hours of night and day, by lot, among themselves.

"August 27 this new regulation was put into practice. More were soon added to this number of intercessors, which was thus increased to seventy-seven, and even the awakened children began a plan similar to this among themselves. Every one carefully observed the hour which had been appointed for them. The intercessors had a weekly meeting, at which notice was given to them of those things which they were to consider special subjects for prayer and remembrance before the Lord.

"The children of both sexes felt a most powerful impulse to prayer, and it was impossible to listen to their infant supplications without being deeply moved and affected. A blessed meeting of the children took place in the evening of the 26th of August, and on the 29th, from the hours of ten o'clock at night until one the following morning a truly affecting scene was witnessed, for the girls from Herrnhut and Berthelsdorf spent these hours in praying, singing and weeping on the

Hutberg. The boys were at the same time engaged in earnest prayer in another place. The spirit of prayer and supplication at that time poured out upon the children was so powerful and efficacious that it is impossible to give an adequate description of it in words. These were truly days of Heavenly enjoyment to the congregation at Herrnhut; all forgot themselves, and things terrestrial and transitory, and longed to be above with Christ their Saviour, in bliss everlasting."

Another eye-witness says:

"I cannot ascribe the cause of the great awakening of the children at Herrnhut to anything but the wonderful outpouring of the Spirit of God upon the communicant congregation assembled on that occasion. The breezes of the Spirit pervaded at that time equally both young and old."

This then is the answer to the question of our chapter - "when the Spirit came." Again we quote from Bishop Evelyn Hasse: "Was there ever in the whole of church history such an astonishing prayer-meeting as that which beginning in 1727, went on one hundred years? It is something absolutely unique. It was known as the 'Hourly Intercession,' and it meant that by relays of Brethren and Sisters prayer without ceasing was made to God for all the work and wants of His church. Prayer of that kind always leads to action. In this case it kindled a burning desire to make Christ's Salvation known to the heathen. It led to the beginning of Modern Foreign Missions. From that one small village community more than one hundred Missionaries who went out in twenty-five years. You will look in vain elsewhere for anything to match it in anything like the same extent." A summary of our chapter may be found in Montgomery's well-known lines:

> They walked with God in Peace and Love,
> But failed with one another;
> While sternly for the Faith they strove,
> Brother fell out with brother;
> But He in whom they put their trust,
> Who knew their frames that they were dust,
> Pitied and healed their weakness.
>
> He found them in His House of Prayer,
> With one accord assembled;
> And so revealed His presence there,

They wept with joy and trembled:
One cup they drank, one bread they brake,
One baptism shared, one language spake,
Forgiving and forgiven.

Then forth they went with tongues of flame,
In one blest theme delighting;
The Love of Jesus and His name,
God's children all uniting;
That Love our theme and watchword still,
The law of love may we fulfill,
And love as we are loved."

Questions for Chapter 2

QUESTION 1:

It is so easy to get together and gossip with our friends and family about concerns and challenges, disagreements and hurts. Is it just as easy to pray about them?

And if it is, do our prayer times become "seasons-of" prayerful gossip?

QUESTION 2:

Describe an example of the last time God "set you to praying" and then showed you "great mercy."

QUESTION 3:

Certainly, Count Zinzendorf was an extremely Godly man. He lived his covenant, "Do Thou be mine, and I will be Thine."

Can we ask, are you willing to covenant something similar? (For example, could you take a blank document and write at the top, "I will be Thine, however You will want me to follow You" And then sign it while it is still blank, letting the Lord fill it in over time?)

QUESTION 4:

In Matthew 16:24 Jesus said that we are to deny ourselves. Are there things that you need to deny yourself?

QUESTION 5:

Zinzendorf knew the power of prayer. He participated in prayer circles and started prayer circles (or prayer societies). Just between you and God, how many prayer meetings do you attend?

Are you not able to attend because of work or other commitments?

Many churches merely do Bible study in lieu of a prayer meeting. Does your church have dedicated times of prayer?

What is stopping you from starting a time of dedicated prayer, in Your Sunday school class, in your church, in your neighborhood or in your home?

QUESTION 6:

"August 13, was preceded and followed by most extraordinary praying." What is meant by "extraordinary" prayer?

How extraordinary is your praying?

QUESTION 7:

Think about your prayers for your loved ones. The statement that Count Zinzendorf was, "A gifted, wealthy, young German nobleman on his knees, agonizing in prayer" has got to challenge the way the you pray for your loved ones!

Between you and God, do you need to be more fervent in prayer for your loved ones?

Then consider covenanting with others, that you would, "together . . . pour out [your] hearts in prayer..."

QUESTION 8:

Motivating the Moravians unto their 100 years of 24-7-365 prayer is the Leviticus 6:13-14 passage that talks about the priest's fire always burning on the alter. Why do you think God wanted that continuous fire?

When you pray, what is your motivation to pray?

Has your motivation been your "needs" or your "desires" and if so, has their focus brought Glory to God?

QUESTION 9:

"Every one carefully observed the hour which had been appointed for them." When was the last time you prayed for a solid hour?

QUESTION 10:

If you are challenged to start a season of prayer, and if it is to bring Glory to God, then why would you ever stop?

"The baptism with the Holy Spirit is a definite experience of which one may and ought to know whether he has received it or not."

"A man may be regenerated by the Holy Spirit and still not be baptized with the Holy Spirit."

"The baptism with the Holy Spirit is an operation of the Holy Spirit distinct from and subsequent and additional to His regenerating work. In regeneration there is an impartation of life, and the one who receives it is saved; in the baptism with the Holy Spirit there is an impartation of power and the one who receives it is fitted for service."

"Baptized with the Holy Spirit," "Filled with the Holy Spirit," "The Holy Ghost fell on them," "The gift of the Holy Ghost was poured out," "Receive the Holy Ghost," "The Holy Ghost came on them," "Gifts of the Holy Ghost," "I send the promise of my Father upon you," "Endued with power from on high," are used in the New Testament to describe one and the same experience."

— *What the Bible Teaches*, R. A. Torrey, D. D.

"At three o'clock we gathered in front of Mr. Moody's mother's home; four hundred and fifty-six of us in all, all men from the eastern colleges. We commenced to climb the mountainside. After we had gone some distance Mr. Moody said: 'I do not think we need to go further. Let us stop here. I can see no reason why we should not kneel down here now and ask God that the Holy Spirit may fall on us as definitely as He fell on the Apostles at Pentecost. Let us pray.' We knelt down on the ground; some of us lay on our faces on the pine-needles. The Holy Ghost fell upon us. It was a wonderful hour. There are many who will never forget it."

— *The Person and Work of the Holy Spirit*, R. A. Torrey, D. D.

Chapter 3

THE SPIRIT'S WITNESS

ONE of the first results of their baptism with the Holy Spirit was the joyful assurance of their pardon and justification. They now experienced as they never had before the force and fullness of the Scripture, "The Spirit Himself beareth witness with our spirit that we are the children of God." Romans 8:16.

One instance of this deserves special mention, as setting forth both their own experience as well as the substance of the message they proclaimed to others.

A little girl, Susanna Kuehnel, eleven years of age, became spiritually awakened. Her dear mother's happy death caused the child to long for a similar living faith and assurance of salvation. She was taught and encouraged to seek the Lord in prayer until the answer came. With strong and ever stronger desire she prayed for the blessed assurance of pardon and peace. Others also united in prayer for her and the historian tells us:

"At one o'clock one morning, while weeping and praying, she broke out into indescribable joy, called to her father, who slept in the adjoining room, and who had, unknown to her, heard all that passed, and cried out: 'Now father, I am become a child of God, and I know also how my mother felt.' She, however, did not only relate to her father what great mercy the Lord had shown her, but out of the abundance of her heart her mouth spake to her companions of His loving kindness towards her, and this she did with such energy that they were deeply affected thereby, and felt themselves powerfully drawn to Jesus."

A venerable Bishop of the Moravian Church tells us that "this little girl, after having spent three days wrestling with God in prayer experienced on August sixth such a divine feeling of the grace of our Saviour, and obtained so clear an assurance of her salvation, that neglecting even the necessary bodily refreshment, she spent the greatest part of that day in proclaiming the praises of her Redeemer." Elsewhere the Bishop calls her, "This little preacher of righteousness." This blessed truth of the Spirit's witness is not such a strange doctrine in our day as it was two centuries ago. Within our memory Mrs. Catherine Booth, the mother of the Salvation Army, instructed her fellow workers as follows in the winning souls:

"Do not tell anybody they are saved. I never do. I leave that for the Holy Ghost to do. I tell them how to get saved. I try to help them to the way of faith. I will bring them up as close as ever I can to the blessed broken body of their Lord, and I will try to show them how willing He is to receive them; and I know that when really they do receive Him, the Spirit of God will tell them quickly enough that they are saved. He will not want any assistance about that. I have proved it in hundreds of cases. Nobody knows the soul but God. Nobody can see the secret windings of the depraved heart but God. Nobody can tell when a full surrender is made but God. Nobody can tell when the right hand is cut off, or the right eye plucked out, but God. Nobody can tell when a soul is whole-hearted but God, and as soon as He sees it, He will tell that soul it is saved."

Moravian experience two centuries ago proves the truth of Mrs. Booth's testimony. The Moravian Pentecost produced the same joyful and victorious assurance of salvation as in apostolic times. They could testify with St. Paul: "Our Gospel came not unto you in word only, but also in power and in the Holy Ghost, and in much assurance." (I. Thess. 1:5.) No better illustration of this can be found than in their life and testimony which led to the conversion of the two famous brothers, John and Charles Wesley. This spiritual experience deserves to rank in depth of knowledge and extent of influence with the historic conversions of St. Paul, St. Augustine, Martin Luther and John Bunyan. It ought to be deeply pondered by every Christian worker who would be a soul-winner. Its thoroughness, regenerating and transforming power deserve our particular consideration. This great story will be told chiefly in the very words of the famous authors and actors themselves.

In the fall of 1735 John and Charles Wesley are on their way to America as Anglican missionaries. A company of Moravian immigrants are also on the vessel. During a terrible storm the danger of ship-wreck was imminent. John Wesley made the following entry in his journal:

"At seven I went to the Germans. 1 had long before observed the great seriousness of their behaviour. Of their humility they had given a continual proof by performing those servile offices for the other passengers, which none of the English would undertake; for which they desired and would receive no pay, saying, 'It was good for their proud hearts,' and 'their loving Saviour had done more for them.' And every day had given them occasion of showing a meekness, which no injury could move. If they were pushed, struck or thrown down, they rose again and went away; but no complaint was found in their mouth. Here was now an opportunity of trying, whether they were delivered from the spirit of fear, as well as from that of pride, anger and revenge. In the midst of the psalm wherewith their service began, the sea broke over, split the main-sail in pieces, covered the ship and poured in between the decks, as if the great deep had already swallowed us up. A terrible screaming began among the English. The Germans calmly sung on. I asked one of them afterwards: 'Were you not afraid?' He answered, 'I thank God, no.' I asked: 'But were not your women and children afraid?' He replied mildly: 'No, our women and children are not afraid to die.'"

After reaching Georgia, Wesley sought spiritual counsel of the Moravian bishop, A. G. Spangenberg. He wrote in his diary, under the date of Feb. 7, 1736: "Mr. Oglethorpe returned from Savannah with Mr. Spangenberg, one of the Pastors of the Germans. I soon found what spirit he was of, and asked his advice with regard to my own conduct. He said:

"'My brother, I must first ask you one or two questions. Have you the witness within yourself? Does the Spirit of God bear witness with your spirit, that you are a child of God?' I was surprised, and knew not what to answer. He observed it and asked: 'Do you know Jesus Christ?' I paused and said: 'I know He is the Saviour of the world.' 'True,' replied he, 'but do you know He has saved you?' I answered: 'I hope He has died to save me.' He only added: 'Do you know yourself?' I said: 'I do.' But I fear they were vain words."

John Wesley's experience with the Christ-like Moravians on board the ship as well as the subsequent probing of his heart by Bishop Spangenberg with reference to the new birth and the assurance of salvation made an abiding impression on his whole life and permanently influenced not only his teaching, but also his behaviour in times of trial and persecution. Returning to England two years later, Wesley wrote in his journal:

"I went to America to convert the Indians; but oh! who shall convert me? Who, what is he that will deliver me from this evil heart of unbelief? I have a fair summer-religion. I can talk well; nay, and believe myself, while no danger is near; but let death look me in the face, and my spirit is troubled. Nor can 1 say 'To die is gain!'

> I have a sin of fear, that when I've spun
> My last thread, I shall perish on the shore.

In Great Britain John and Charles Wesley became quite intimately acquainted with the Moravian Brethren. Peter Boehler, later a leading bishop in the Moravian Church, was particularly blessed in his efforts to lead John Wesley into the full light of the Gospel. Under date of March 4, 1738, Wesley made the following entry in his diary:

"I found my brother at Oxford recovering from his pleurisy; and with him Peter Boehler: by whom (in the hand of the great God) 1 was, on Sunday, the 5th, clearly convinced of unbelief; of the want of that faith whereby alone we are saved. Immediately it struck into my mind, 'Leave off preaching. How can you preach to others who have not faith yourself ?' I asked Boehler whether he thought I should leave it off, or not. He answered, 'By no means.' I asked: 'But what can I preach?' He said: 'Preach faith till you have it; and then, because you have it, you will preach faith.' Accordingly, Monday, 6, 1 began preaching this new doctrine, though my soul started back from the work. The first person to whom I offered salvation by faith alone, was a prisoner under sentence of death."

At length he himself was led into the full assurance of salvation. His own testimony in this matter is conclusive. In his diary we read:

"Wednesday, May 3, 1738. My brother had a long and particular conversation with Peter Boehler. And it now pleased God to open his eyes; so that he also saw clearly, what was the nature of that one true living faith, whereby alone 'through grace we are saved.'

"Wednesday, May 24. In the evening I went very unwillingly to a society in Aldersgate street, where one was reading Luther's preface to the Epistle to the Romans. About a quarter before nine, while he was describing the change which God works in the heart through faith in Christ, I felt my heart strangely warmed. I felt I did trust in Christ, Christ alone, for salvation; and an assurance was given me, that He had taken away my sins, even mine, and saved me from the law of sin and death.

"Friday, May 26. My soul continued in peace, but yet in heaviness, because of manifold temptations. I asked Mr. Telchig, the Moravian, what to do. He said: "You must not fight with them as you did before, but flee from them the moment they appear, and take shelter in the wounds of Jesus."

The Methodists and Moravians in those days often met together for Bible-study and prayer. The great preacher, George Whitefield, refers to a Moravian Love Feast and prayer-meeting in his journal. His biographer tells us:

"Whitefield began the New Year (1739) as gloriously as he ended that which had just expired. He received Sacrament, preached twice, expounded twice, attended a Moravian Love Feast in Fetter Lane, where he spent the whole night in prayer to God, psalms and thanksgiving; and then pronounced 'this to be the happiest New Year's Day he had ever seen.'

"This Love Feast at Fetter Lane was a memorable one. Besides about sixty Moravians, there were present not fewer than seven of the Oxford Methodists, namely, John and Charles Wesley, George Whitefield, Wesley Hall, Benjamin Ingham, Charles Kinchin and Richards Hutchins, all of them ordained clergymen of the Church of England. Wesley writes: 'About three in the morning, as we were continuing instant in prayer, the power of God came mightily upon us, insomuch that many cried for exceeding joy, and many fell to the ground. As soon as we were recovered a little from that awe and amazement at the presence of His Majesty, we broke out with one voice-'We Praise Thee, O God; we acknowledge Thee to be the Lord!'"

One of Wesley's first converts was his dear old mother, the "Godly Susanna," whom some one has called "the mother of Methodism and of nineteen children besides." The following is from John Wesley's journal:

"Monday, Sept. 3. 1 talked largely with my mother, who told me that till a short time since she had scarce heard such a thing mentioned as the having forgiveness of sins now, or God's Spirit bearing witness with our spirit; much less did she imagine that this was the common privilege of all true believers. 'Therefore,' said she, 'I never durst ask it for myself. But two or three weeks ago, while my son, Hall, was pronouncing those words, in delivering the cup to me, 'The Blood of our lord Jesus Christ, which was given for thee,' the words struck through my heart, and I know God for Christ's sake has forgiven me all my sins.'"

The conversion of John and Charles Wesley marks an epoch in the history of Protestantism. In a recent sermon on John Wesley, Dr. S. Parkes Cadman, president of the Federal Council of Churches, spoke as follows:

"On the Westward trip to Georgia he fell in with some Moravian Brethren, who revealed to Wesley his need of a personal and regenerating contact with Christ. He never rested until he found that contact. It is not too much to say that what happened in that little meeting-house in Aldersgate street on May 24, 1738, changed the political and religious destinies of English-speaking Protestantism. By God's help he relit the expiring fires of religion. It was his conversion which crowned his preparation. Twice born, and both times most nobly born, he cannot be understood apart from the training of Epworth Rectory and his transformation in Aldersgate Street, London."

Wesley's own estimate of the revival which resulted in his conversion was remarkably prophetic. When his spiritual father, Peter Boehler, who was nine years his junior, left England after a stay of several months, Wesley recorded in his journal:

"Peter Boehler left London to embark for Carolina. Oh what a work hath God begun since his coming into England! Such an one as shall never come to an end, till Heaven and earth pass away!"

A few extracts from Peter Boehler's letters to Count Zinzendorf may well close this chapter on the witness of the Spirit:

"The English people made a wonderful to do about me; and though I could not speak much English they were always wanting me to tell them about our Saviour, His blood and wounds, and the forgiveness of sins.

"On the 28th of February I traveled with the brothers John and Charles Wesley from London to Oxford. The older of the two, John, is an amiable man; he acknowledges that he does not yet really know the Saviour, but is willing to be instructed. He loves us sincerely. His brother, with whom you frequently conversed last year when you were in London, is greatly troubled in mind, and does not know how to begin to learn to know the Saviour.

"I heard John Wesley preach. I could understand all he said, but it was not what 1 wished to hear. Hence I took four of my English brethren, among them Wolf, to see him, that they might tell him their experience and show him that the Saviour receives sinners quickly and willingly. One by one they began to unfold to Wesley what they had experienced. Wolf, especially, a new convert, spoke most feelingly and with great power of the grace which he had received. Wesley and others who were with him listened in blank amazement. I then asked Wesley what he thought of such experiences. He answered that four instances were not enough and could not convince him. 1 replied that I could bring forward eight more cases of the same kind in London. After a little while he rose and said: 'Let us sing Hymn 456, "My Soul Before Thee Prostrate Lies." ' During the singing he frequently wiped his eyes, and immediately after called me into his bedroom and confessed that he was now convinced of the truth of what I had told him about faith and would no longer dispute it, but that he had not attained to this grace. How was he to secure such faith? He had not sinned as grossly as others. I replied, that not to believe in the Saviour was sin enough, and exhorted him to seek Christ until he had found Him as his Saviour. I was strongly moved to pray with him and called on the Redeemer to have mercy on this sinner. After the prayer Wesley remarked that when the gift of saving faith would once be his, he would preach upon no other subject.

"I had another affectionate conversation with John Wesley. He informed me of the opposition he had met with on the part of some orthodox ministers to whom he had made known his conviction that he did not as yet possess true, saving faith. He asked me what he ought to do. Should he tell his state to the people to whom he preached? I answered that I could give him no rule in this respect, that he must follow the promptings of the Saviour; but I earnestly begged him not to look for the Saviour's grace as far off and in the future, but to believe that it was present, nigh to him, that the heart of Jesus was open and His love to him very great. He wept bitterly and asked me to pray with him. I can truly affirm that he is a poor, heart-broken sinner, hungering after a better righteousness, than that which he has thus far had, even the righteousness of Jesus Christ. In the evening he preached on 1. Cor. 1:23-24, 'We Preach Christ Crucified,' etc. He had more than four thousand hearers and spoke in such a way that all were amazed. They had never before heard such doctrines from his lips. His first words were: 'I sincerely confess myself unworthy to preach to you of the Crucified Jesus.' All poor sinners could appreciate this, all who felt their own misery. Many were awakened by this sermon!"

Thus far Peter Boehler. We cannot but exclaim: What a truly noble soul John Wesley was!

No wonder he preached in demonstration of the Spirit and of power and caused more than 130,000 persons to rally around him during his lifetime. Eighty years after Wesley's death Methodism could boast of twelve million adherents; today of nearly thirty millions. Dean Farrar has well said: "The Evangelical movement, the Oxford movement, even the recent enthusiasm. of the Salvation Army are traceable to Wesley's example, and to the convictions which he inspired." Bishop Lightfoot also testified that "The Salvationists, taught by John Wesley, have learned and have taught the Church again, the lost secret of the compulsion of human souls to the Saviour."

We stand in spirit around the death-bed of John Wesley. For nearly three score years he has preached Christ and practiced holiness. He has traveled on his ceaseless round of duty some 4,500 miles annually, and preached two or more sermons every day, often to immense audiences. At the age of 86 he records an address delivered to a congregation of 25,000. Now the old hero and valiant soldier of the Cross is facing "the last enemy." We hear him whisper again and again:

I the chief of sinners am,
But Jesus died for me.

We recognize this confession of faith, both in its substance and phraseology. The songs and sermons of the Moravian Brethren have it as their constant theme. Amongst them Wesley had learned and received this saving truth. His friend and fellow-worker, "the holy" John Fletcher, Methodism's chief saint, had shortly before departed this life with the dying testimony:

> I nothing have, I nothing am,
> My treasure's in the bleeding Lamb,
> Both now and evermore."

We may speak with the tongues of men and of angels, we may have the gift of prophecy and understand all mysteries and all knowledge, we may have all faith, so that we could remove mountains, we may bestow all our goods to feed the poor and give our bodies to be burned,-in the hour of death and in the day of judgment, nothing will avail unless we have learned in the school of the Holy Ghost.

> I the chief of sinners am,
> But Jesus died for me.

Questions for Chapter 3

QUESTION 1:

Noting R. A. Torrey's words before this chapter even started, can you say that you have been "fitted for service" not merely regenerated as have been all Christians?

QUESTION 2:

Are the words "happy death" foreign to your way of viewing death?

Why or why not?

QUESTION 3:

Remembering of the Moravian's lack of fear, and their statement that "...our women and children are not afraid to die," can you do an assessment of your family and answer the question, are they afraid to die?

QUESTION 4:

So, ask yourself, as Mr. Spangenberg asked Wesley, "Does the Spirit of God bear witness with your spirit, that you are a child of God?"

This question is the essence of the assurance of salvation and it must be seriously considered.

QUESTION 5:

    After John Wesley is saved, he is told by Mr. Telchig to "not fight with [temptations] as [he] did before, but flee from them the moment they appear, and take shelter in the wounds of Jesus."

    Looking into James 4:7, which word best describes how this Moravian is advising John Wesley to live — submitting or resisting?

    Why did you choose the one you did?

QUESTION 6:

    Our author tells us, "The Methodists and Moravians in those days often met together for Bible-study and prayer." Whom else do you meet with, for Bible-study and prayer?

    Why or why not?

QUESTION 7:

    The epoch event in Protestantism, per our author, was the conversion of John and Charles Wesley. Has there been an epoch conversion in your family, your mother, your father, another?

    Is it possible that your conversion is the epoch event in your family?

QUESTION 8:

     To John Wesley, his entire life was summed up in 11 words: "I the chief of sinners am, but Jesus died for me." How would you sum up your life?

QUESTION 9:

     Thirty million people (as of the writing of this book) have been influenced by John Wesley's conversion. Who are you influencing? Who are you asking God to influence through you?

QUESTION 10:

This chapter ends with the death of John Wesley. And in another book, we are told that at his death he left: six, 1-lb notes, six, silver spoons, a handful of books, a Geneva gown and one more thing. What was it? Oh yes, he left the Methodist church. What are you leaving behind?

"The glorified Christ is He who baptizes with the Holy Spirit. When the Lord Jesus Himself was baptized with the Spirit, it was because He had humbled Himself and offered Himself to take part in John's baptism of repentance-a baptism for sinners-in Jordan. Even so, when He took upon Himself the work of Redemption, He received the Holy Spirit to fit Him for His work from that hour till on the Cross "He offered Himself without spot to God." Do you desire that this Glorified Christ should baptize you with the Holy Spirit? Offer yourself then to Him for His service, to further His great work of making known to sinners the love of the Father. God help us to understand what a great thing it is to receive the Holy Spirit with power from the Glorified Jesus. Have you laid hold of it? The abundant life is neither more nor less than the full life of Christ as the Crucified, the Risen, the Glorified One, who baptizes with the Holy Ghost, and reveals Himself in our hearts and lives, as Lord of all within us."

— *The Prayer-Life*, Andrew Murray

"Before we go to our knees to receive the Baptism of Fire, let me beg of you to see to it that your souls are in harmony with the will and purpose of the Holy Spirit whom you seek. See to it that the channel of communication, by which the baptism of the Holy Spirit must be received, be kept open. I heard of some people the other day who could not get any water. They turned the tap repeatedly, but no water came. They sent to the office of the company, who sent a man to examine the connections and fittings, but all was right. Plenty of water in the reservoir; pipes, taps and connections all right, but no water. At last they pulled up the pipe and found a mouse in it. It is no use turning the tap, praying, singing or even believing, if there is something you are holding back or refusing to do-some idol, something about which you feel condemned, but which you refuse to give up, something in the pipe. Perhaps some trumpery, contemptible thing. Out with it; give it no rest; give it up. Destroy your idols and hindrances and stoppages, with an everlasting destruction. Let there be free communication between you and God. Let all go, and you shall be flooded before you rise from your knees; the world shall feel the power of it, and God shall have all the glory."

— *Salvation Soldiery*, William Booth

Chapter 4

WITNESS UNTO ME

YE shall receive power when the Holy Ghost is come upon you; and ye shall be witnesses unto me both in Jerusalem and in all Judea, and in Samaria, and unto the uttermost part of the earth." Acts 1:8.

One mark of a genuine baptism with the Holy Ghost is the exaltation of Christ. "He shall glorify me," said Jesus with reference to the promised Paraclete. (John 16:14.) One result of Pentecost in apostolic days was the determination "to know nothing among men save Jesus Christ and Him crucified." (Acts 2:23; 3:15; 4:10; 1. Cor. 2:2; etc., etc.)

This is exactly what happened two centuries ago in Herrnhut. They were all filled with the Holy Spirit and became witnesses of Christ and Him crucified. Their theology became Christology. Their creed was in one word, "the Cross." One of their number, John Cennick, truly set this forth in the stanza:

> Christ is our Master Lord and God,
> The fullness of the Three in One;
> His life, death, righteousness and blood,
> Our faith's foundation are alone,
> His Godhead and His Death shall be
> Our theme to all eternity.

The Baptism with the Holy Spirit caused the Renewed Moravian Church to see no man save Jesus only. Their spiritual vision became so keen that they could "see Him who is invisible." (Heb. 11:27). The form in which He appeared to them most frequently was when He was "led as a Lamb to the slaughter, wounded for their transgressions and bruised for their iniquities."

In this divine presence of their bleeding and dying Lord they were overwhelmed with their own sinfulness and with His more abounding grace. Hushed were their controversies and quarrels; crucified were their passions and pride as they gazed upon the agonies of their "expiring God." With the Apostle they learned to die daily unto the world, the flesh and the devil, and to live for Him who died for them.

Henceforth their one passion was to gaze upon the King in His beauty and to proclaim the "slaughtered Lamb" as the "chief among ten thousand and the one altogether lovely." They did exactly what they sang:

> Then will 1 tell to sinners 'round,
> What a dear Saviour I have found;
> I'll point to the atoning Blood
> And say 'Behold the way to God.'"

Their prayers, their litanies, their hymns, their conversation and their sermons had one theme, viz., the wounds, the blood and death of Jesus. Their great leader, Count Zenzendorf, set this forth most clearly in his famous hymn:

> The Saviour's blood and righteousness
> My beauty is, my glorious dress;
> Thus well arrayed, 1 need not fear,
> When in His presence I appear.
>
> The holy, spotless Lamb of God,
> Who freely gave His life and blood,
> For all my numerous sins to atone,
> I for my Lord and Saviour own.
>
> In Him I trust for evermore;
> He hath expunged the dreadful score
> Of all my guilt; this done away,
> I need not fear the judgment-day.
>
> Therefore my Saviour's blood and death
> Are here the substance of my faith;
> And shall remain, when I'm called hence,
> My only hope and confidence."

How many thousands have been brought to Jesus by this hymn, eternity alone can reveal.

Moravian sermons were just as full of Christ and His atonement as were Moravian hymns. In one of Count Zinzendorf's letters we find the following declaration:

"Our method in proclaiming salvation is this: To point out to every heart the Loving Lamb, who died for us and although He was the Son of God offered Himself for our sins, as his God, his Mediator between God and man, his throne of grace, his example, his brother, his preacher of the law, his comforter, his confessor, his Saviour, in short, his all in all; by the preaching of His blood, and of His love unto death even the death of the cross; never, either in the discourse or in the argument, to digress even for a quarter of an hour from the Loving Lamb; to name no virtue except in Him, and from Him and on His account; to preach no commandment except faith in Him; no other justification but that He atoned for us; no other sanctification but the privilege to sin no more; no other happiness but to be near Him, to think of Him and do His pleasure; no other self-denial but to be deprived of Him and His blessings; no other calamity but to displease Him; no other life but in Him."

It was of such Christo-Centric preaching that Prof. Binnie in a series of lectures in St. George's Free Church, Edinburgh, recently declared: "Count Zinzendorf preached the gospel himself with remarkable simplicity and power to an age which greatly needed it-an age which needed to be called off from unprofitable controversies that were wasting its vital energies, and to be roused to open its heart to the message of reconciliation through Christ. This evangelical message Zinzendorf not only preached in person to men of all ranks in half the countries of Europe and amongst the colonists in America, but he sent it out to the heathen also for whom no man cared. He was a great Evangelist and Missionary."

Of Zinzendorf as a preacher we have the following pen picture by one of his contemporaries, Count Schrautenbach:

"He hardly ever read any books besides the Bible. He never wrote his sermons; but their effect was very great. His discourses resembled soliloquies uttered in the presence of an auditory. Never have sermons afforded a truer reflection of the character, genius and innermost thoughts of the speaker. When we hear him, we see his whole soul laid bare before us. His personal convictions could be felt in all his words. His voice was robust, pleasant, sonorous and capable of fine modulation and expression, both when he spoke and when he sang. Life, soul and harmony pervaded all he said and did. His countenance was sublime and capable of great expression. His forehead was broad and ample; his eyes dark-blue, full of fire and in constant motion; his lips were well-formed and calmly closed, and his glance was quick and penetrating. He was respectful towards everyone with whom he had to do; although all felt and acknowledged his superiority."

As a soul-winner the Wachovia Moravian well says:

"There never lived a man since the days of Christ and the Apostles who had more gift in dealing with souls than Count Zinzendorf. He was a great believer in sudden grace. We've just come across a brief quotation of what he said upon this subject. It runs thus:

"When the Spirit of God has at some time enlightened us with a sudden lightning flash, we must afterward not extinguish the flame nor destroy it nor hide it."

"His own experiences and those of others bore out the truth of the saying. His own purpose in life was fixed in a moment. In a picture gallery he was looking at a Christ head with a crown of thorns and a bleeding face and underneath he read the inscription, 'This I have done for thee; what hast thou done for Me?' and in an instant his mind was made up as to what he would do for a lifetime. And a very fruitful life it was because by direct or indirect influence millions of souls have been brought into the kingdom of God."

Count Zinzendorf knew very well that all who will live godly in Christ Jesus must suffer opposition and persecution. No one experienced this in modern times more than he. As one of the chief disturbers of the devil's kingdom he was singled out as a shining target by the enemy of souls. But none of these lies, slanders, trials and tribulations moved him in the slightest. On the contrary he encouraged and exhorted his brethren in the ministry and fellow-workers to be awakening preachers at all costs of personal popularity. In one of his addresses he told them:

"Let every minister rest assured that if he desires to enjoy ease, and have things go on smoothly in his congregation, revivals and conversions dare not take place. For as soon as these occur, the devil is loose, no matter how decently and in order everything may be conducted."

"In an Apostolic church a gentle mode of teaching is appropriate. But if, in a mixed congregation, there are no sons of thunder, no Elijahs, the people go to sleep."

"The style of preaching, to which many congregations are forced to listen, is entirely too philosophical, cold, logical, abstruse, cautious and reserved. A preacher, in order to be truly successful, must be bold, mighty through God to the pulling down of strongholds, casting down imaginations and every high thing that exalts itself against the knowledge of God, and to the bringing into captivity every thought to the obedience of Christ. He must bear down all opposition, tear down the fair but false fabrics of formalism and self-righteousness; overturn, burn, and destroy every wrong foundation, together with its superstructure, ere it is possible to build up a spiritual house unto the Lord."

The sum and substance of the Gospel which these Spirit-filled Moravians preached in all parts of the earth may be learned from the following sentences taken almost at random from Zinzendorf's sermons:

"Christians are God's people, begotten by His Spirit, obedient to Him, enkindled by His fire; His blood is their glory."

"In order to preach aright, take three looks before every sermon; one at thine own sinfulness; another at the depth of human wretchedness all around thee; and a third at the love of God in Christ Jesus; so that empty of self, and full of compassion towards thy fellowmen, thou mayest be enabled to administer God's comfort to souls."

"I am, as ever, a poor sinner, a captive of eternal love, running by the side of His triumphal chariot, and I have no desire to be anything else as long as I live."

"The whole earth is the Lord's; men's souls are His; I am debtor to all."

"It is not enough to rely upon God's grace in general; we must build upon the grace of God in the blood of Jesus."

"In every degree and phase of our spiritual life and growth and service the blood of Jesus is indispensable."

"The blood of Christ is not only the sovereign remedy for sin; it is also the chief nourishment of the Christian life."

"The Spirit comes to us by the way of the blood for full salvation."

"Our preaching of the wounds and blood of Jesus may not produce many sudden conversions, but they will be thorough and lasting."

This was also the Gospel which the young graduate of Jena University, Peter Boehler, preached in England which resulted in the conversion of many Oxford students and professors as well as ordained clergymen of the Church of England and Scotland. Nearly one century later that prince of Scotch preachers, Dr. Thomas Chalmers, wrote a long article in the Eclectic Review on The Moravians in which he put the stamp of his approval on their theology and Gospel in the following striking sentences:

"The efficacy of the Bible alone upon simple and unfurnished minds is a fact; and the finest examples of it are to be found in almost every page of the annals of Moravianism. When the Apostle Paul went about among Greeks and Barbarians, charged with the message of salvation to all who would listen and believe, he preached nothing but Jesus Christ and Him Crucified. Neither do the Moravians; and the faith which attends the word of their testimony, how foolish and fanatical soever it may appear in the eyes of worldly men, proves it to be the power of God and the wisdom of God unto salvation. It is another evidence of the foolishness of God being wiser than men, and the weakness of God being stronger than men. However wonderful it may be, yet such is the fact, that a savage, when spoken to on the subject of his soul, of sin and of the Saviour has his attention more easily compelled, and his resistence more effectually subdued than when he is addressed upon any other subject of moral or economical instruction. And this is precisely the way in which Moravians have gone to work. They preached the peculiar tenets of the New Testament at the very outset. They gained converts through that faith which comes by hearing. It is well that the Moravians have risen into popular admiration. This will surely give weight to their own testimony about their own matters. One of their members, Bishop Spangenberg, has published an account of the manner in which the United Brethren preach the Gospel.

We shall subjoin a few extracts:"

(Here follow many pages of quotations from Bishop Spangenberg's book, one of which is the following:)

"About thirty years ago, when I lived in North America, I sometimes got the brethren together that were in the service, in order that I might converse with them about their labors. Johannes, an Indian Chief, who had formerly been a very wicked man, but was now thoroughly converted and was our fellow laborer in the congregations gathered from among the heathen, happened to be just then on a visit with us, and also came to our Conference. He was a man that had excellent gifts and was a bold confessor of what he knew to be true. As we were speaking with one another about the heathen he said, among other things:

"Brethren, I have been a heathen and am grown old among them. I know therefore very well how it is with the heathen. A preacher came once to us, desiring to instruct us, and began by proving to us that there was a God. On which we said to him, 'Well, and dost thou think we are ignorant of that? Now, go again whence thou camest.' Another preacher came another time, and would instruct us, saying, 'You must not steal, nor drink too much, nor lie,' etc., etc. We answered him: 'Fool, that thou art: Dost thou think we do not know that? Go and learn it first thyself and teach the people thou belongest to not to do these things. For who are greater drunkards or thieves or liars, than thine own people?' Thus we sent him away also. Some time after this, Christian Henry Rauch, one of the Moravian Brethren, came to me into my hut and sat down by me. The contents of his discourse to me were nearly these: 'I come to thee in the name of the Lord of Heaven and Earth. He acquaints thee that He would gladly save thee, and rescue thee from the miserable state in which thou liest. To this end He became a man, hath given His life for mankind and shed His blood for them,' etc. Upon this he lay down upon a board in my hut and fell asleep, being fatigued with his journey. I thought within myself: What manner of man is this? There he lies and sleeps so sweetly. I might kill him and throw him out into the forest Who would care? But he is unconcerned. However, I could not get rid of his words. They continually recurred to me; and though I went to sleep yet I dreamed of the blood which Christ had shed for me. I thought 'this is very strange,' and went to interpret to the other

Indians the words of Christian Henry. Thus, through the grace of God, the awakening among us took place. I tell you therefore, brethren, preach to the heathen Christ and his blood and death, if you would wish to produce a blessing among them."

Shortly after publishing this famous article on The Moravians in the Eclectic Review, Dr. Chalmers wrote to a dear personal friend: "I beg you to dwell much and affectionately on the great peculiarities of the Gospel-Christ our propitiation, Christ our sanctification, and Christ in us the hope of glory."

Count Zinzendorf put the same exhortation into poetry and sang:

A messenger of peace
No higher pleasure knows,
Than to direct the human race
To Jesus' Cross;
He points to Jesus' wounds,
And precious cleansing blood;
The source, whence life to us redounds,
The fount of good.

Witnesses for Jesus and of Jesus was what every Moravian was in those great revival decades. The secret of Methodist success as given by John Wesley applies equally to the Moravians, viz., "We are all at it, and at it always."

The following editorial in the Wachovia Moravian shows us a typical Moravian of that Pentecostal age:

"There was a Countess several generations ago who had led what the world calls a very merry life. She was highly situated in society, connected in close friendship with kings and emperors and princes. She was a welcome center on brilliant occasions of dance and festivity in view of her brilliant gifts and witty conversation, and yet she became afflicted with an incurable melancholy. None of her amusements and recreations satisfied her any longer and everything before her and around her seemed dark indeed.

Under the old custom of measuring shoes for the feet of their wearers, an humble Moravian shoemaker was one day invited into her presence. As he opened the door, she was struck by the remarkable cheerfulness which shone forth from his face. She watched him closely while he knelt at his humble task of measuring for the shoes and was deeply impressed by the unaffected happiness written upon his very looks. She was led to say to him, 'You seem to be a very happy man.' 'Yes,' he said, 'I am very happy all the time.' 'You are very different from me,' the high-born lady said. 'I am just as miserable as anybody could be. Would you mind telling me what makes you so happy?' 'No,' the Moravian shoemaker said, 'I'll be glad to tell you. Jesus has forgiven my sins. He forgives me every day and He loves me and that makes me happy through all the hours."

"The job was finished and the man went away. But the Countess thought over what he said. Thought led to prayer and prayer to conviction and conviction swiftly introduced her into a joyful faith in the shoemaker's Saviour. She became a great witness for Christ among titled people and especially at the court of the emperor of Russia, Alexander I., her intimate friend.

"It was this joy of their faith suddenly born in their souls by the gift of God's Spirit in the communion hour, Wednesday, August 13, 1727, that made the Moravian brothers and sisters glad to come to this country (America) and many others, facing all the hardships and difficulties of a new, strange land. It was this joy that led them willingly into the deep forests of Indian abode and made them so successful as missionaries among the very wildest savages.

"It is this Christian joy to which even some preachers have not yet attained and many members have not yet reached, upon which the Moravian Church must depend for its future influence everywhere and thus the Word of God be fulfilled in a new century, as it was two centuries ago. 'The joy of the Lord is your strength.'"

"It was the sight of this joy which the Moravians had in the midst of the hurricane when the vessel was on the point of sinking into the wild sea that so impressed the Brethren John and Charles Wesley as to lead to that deep personal experience of grace upon which the Methodist Church was founded: and the impression that this Christian joy has made upon them it has made even upon countless savages in darkened heathen lands and is the ultimate reason why the Moravian Church among the many larger denominations still continues to exist."

Questions for Chapter 4

QUESTION 1:

"One mark of a genuine baptism of the Holy Ghost is the exaltation of Christ." When was the last time you shared Christ with a lost person?

QUESTION 2:

Were you amazed by these words like I was? They said that they would, "preach no commandment except faith in Him."

Amazing, isn't it? Especially in our world. We SOOO want to tell people what to do in every area of their life, but what was the Christo-Centric focus of The Moravians?

QUESTION 3:

Can you think of "unprofitable controversies that [are] wasting vital energies" in your denomination?

How about in your church?

How about in your home?

And how about in your heart?

QUESTION 4:

When you speak to others about the spiritual things, do they see your "whole soul laid bare before" them?

QUESTION 5:

Count Zinzendorf said that "all who will live godly in Christ Jesus must suffer opposition and persecution." Do you think that still applies to today?

If so, without comparing yourself to the Moravians, where and how are you suffering opposition and/or persecution?

QUESTION 6:

What did Count Zinzendorf mean when he said, "Christians are...enkindled by His fire..."

QUESTION 7:

What did Count Zinzendorf mean when he said "The blood of Christ is not only the sovereign remedy for sin; it is also the chief nourishment of the Christian life?"

QUESTION 8:

What were the three "peculiar tenets of the New Testament" that The Moravians taught?

Answer: The subject of his S_____,

of S_____

and of the S_____

QUESTION 9:

In your normal course of the day, do people stop you and ask you "what makes you so happy?"

QUESTION 10:

Think of your most recent hurricane. Did you exhibit "Christian joy?"

In what way did you or did you not?

How could have handled this hurricane differently?

"I have written and preached much on the Holy Spirit, for the knowledge of Him has been the most vital fact of my experience. I owe everything to the gift of Pentecost.... I came across a prophet, heard a testimony, and set out to seek I knew not what. I knew that it was a bigger thing and a deeper need than I had ever known. It came along the line of duty, and I entered in through a crisis of obedience. When it came I could not explain what had happened, but I was aware of things unspeakable and full of glory. Some results were immediate. There came into my soul a deep peace, a thrilling joy, and a new sense of power. My mind was quickened. I felt that I had received a new faculty of understanding. Every power was alert. Either illumination took the place of logic, or reason became intuitive. My bodily powers also were quickened. There was a new sense of spring and vitality, a new power of endurance, and a strong man's exhilaration in big things. Things began to happen. What we had failed to do by strenuous endeavor came to pass without labor. It was as when the Lord Jesus stepped into the boat that with all their rowing had made no progress, immediately the ship was at the land whither they went. It was gloriously wonderful."

— Dr. Samuel Chadwick, of Cliff College, England.

"Never shall I forget the gain to conscious faith and peace which came to my soul, not long after a first decisive and appropriating view of the Crucified Lord as the sinner's sacrifice of peace, from a more intelligent and conscious hold upon the living and most gracious personality of the Holy Spirit through whose mercy the soul had got that blessed view. It was a new development of insight into the love of God. It was a new contact as it were with the inner and eternal movements of redeeming goodness, a new discovery in divine resources."

— C. G. Moule, Bishop of Durham.

"Often have I said to myself, as I have read Moravian history, and felt the sweet strength of the Moravian literature of devotion and praise: Si non essem Anglicanus utinem fierem Moravus; 'If I were not of the English Church I would fain be of the Moravian'."

— Bishop Moule, of Durham.

Chapter 5

A NEW SONG

"HE hath put a new song in my mouth, even praise unto our God." (Psalm 40:3)

"Be filled with the Spirit: speaking to yourselves in psalms, and hymns, and spiritual songs, singing and making melody in your heart to the Lord." (Ephesians 5:18-19)

The baptism with the Holy Spirit upon our fathers two centuries ago produced such a spiritual floodtide of sacred song as had not been experienced in the Christian Church before or since. The majority of our best church hymns may be traced to this outpouring of the Holy Spirit. Praise to Christ, adoration of Him as God, proclamation of His virtues and work are their constant theme.

These were true hymns. They are generally prayers to Christ. This may almost be considered a Moravian peculiarity: their prayers are generally addressed to their Saviour. Seldom do we find a Moravian hymn or prayer in those days directed to the Father. Thus honoring the Son they honored the Father who had sent Him as well as the Holy Spirit whose chief mission it was to glorify Him. Indeed nearly all of our great hymns are prayers addressed to Jesus. A truly converted Catholic or Protestant, Calvinist or Lutheran, Moravian or Arminian, Baptist or Quaker, when he is baptized with the Holy Ghost and with fire often breaks out into sacred song and it is generally prayer or praise addressed to Jesus.

This was preeminently the case in Herrnhut two centuries ago. The chief singer of the period was the godly young nobleman, Count Zinzendorf. He became the prince of German hymn-writers. We have already referred to his great song which John Wesley translated:

> Jesus, Thy Blood and Righteousness,
> My beauty are my glorious dress;
> Midst flaming worlds in these arrayed
> With joy I can lift up my head.

Justification by faith and the new birth are to be found at the cross of Jesus. Here also does the believer grow in true holiness and obtains the baptism of the Holy Spirit. This is set forth in another of Zinzendorf's great hymns, also translated by John Wesley:

I thirst, Thou wounded Lamb of God,
To wash me in Thy cleansing blood;
To dwell within Thy wounds; then pain
Is sweet; and life or death is gain.

What are our works but sin and death,
Till Thou Thy quickening Spirit breathe!
Thou bidst each good within us move,
O wondrous grace! O boundless love!

How blest are they who still abide
Close sheltered in Thy bleeding side!
Who life and strength from thence derive,
And by Thee move, and in Thee live!

Take my poor heart and let it be
Forever closed to all but Thee!
Seal Thou my breast and let me bear
That pledge of love forever there.

Having received such abundant spiritual baptism it is not be wondered at that many of their hymns were also addressed to or occupied with the Holy Spirit. Again we quote several stanzas from Count Zinzendorf on this subject:

To Thee, God Holy Ghost, we pray,
Who lead'st us in the Gospel way,
Those precious gifts on us bestow,
Which from our Saviour's merits flow.

Thou Heavenly Teacher, Thee we praise,
For Thy instruction, power and grace,
To love the Father, Who doth own
Us as His children in the Son.

Most gracious Comforter, we pray,
O lead us further every day:

Thy unction to us all impart,
Preserve and sanctify each heart!

Till we in Heaven shall take our seat,
Instruct us often to repeat
"Abba, our Father"; and to be
With Christ in union constantly.

Next in ability, influence, piety and spiritual power to Count Zinzendorf was Bishop Spangenberg, Wesley's first Moravian teacher. He also wrote a number of hymns, in one of which he prays to the Holy Ghost as follows:

The Church of Christ, that He hath hallowed here
To be His house, is scattered far and near,
In North, and South, and East and West abroad;
And yet in earth and heaven, through Christ, her Lord,
The Church is one.

One member knoweth not another here,
And yet their fellowship is true and near;
One is their Saviour, and their Father one;
One Spirit rules them, and among them none
Lives to himself.

They live to Him Who bought them with His blood,
Baptized them with His Spirit, pure and good;
And in true faith and ever-burning love,
Their hearts and hopes ascend, to seek above
The eternal good.

O Spirit of the Lord, all life is Thine;
Now fill Thy Church with life and power divine,
That many children may be born to Thee,
And spread Thy knowledge like the boundless sea,
To Christ's great praise.

Christian women and young people also were filled with the Spirit and prophesied. Their prayers and praises often found expression in Psalms and hymns and spiritual songs. Countess Zinzendorf composed the beautiful hymn beginning:

Reach out Thy scepter, King of Love,
Let us Thy royal favor prove!

The second stanza is a particular prayer for holiness and power from on high:

O ground us deeper still in Thee,
And let us Thy true followers be;
And when of Thee we testify,
Fill Thou our hearts with heavenly joy;
May Thy blest Spirit all our souls inspire,
And set each cold and lifeless heart on fire.

One of the many who experienced the new birth and the assurance of salvation through Zinzendorf's preaching was Louise Van Hayn. She also wrote a number of hymns, one of which is a favorite in the American Moravian Church:

Jesus makes my heart rejoice,
I'm His sheep and know His Voice.

Amongst the youth who composed songs of praise and adoration may be mentioned Count Zinzeiidorf's son, Christian Renatus. Perhaps his best lines are the following:

Lamb of God, Thou shalt remain forever
Of our songs the only theme;
For Thy boundless love, Thy grace and favor,
We will praise Thy saving Name;
That for our transgressions Thou wast wounded,
Shall by us in nobler strains be sounded,
When we, perfected in love,
Once shall join the Church above.

Another young man whose heart was set on fire with the love of Jesus was John de Watteville, Zinzendorf's son-in-law. His best known hymn is the one beginning:

Jesus, Thyself to us reveal,
Grant that we may not only feel
Some drawings of Thy grace,
But in communion with Thee live,

And daily from Thy death derive
The needful strength to run our race.

One of the most remarkable and gifted youth of this great revival period was Christian Frederick Gregor. The brief biographical note in our Moravian Hymn Book indicates his versatile genius as follows:

"Financial agent of Zinzendorf, organist at Herrnhut, member of Unity's Elders Conference and Bishop." His hymns are all deeply spiritual. Perhaps his famous passion hymn is a favorite in all Moravian congregations. The two best known stanzas are the following:

In this sepulchral Eden
The tree of life I've found;
Here is my treasure hidden,
I tread on holy ground;
Ye sick, ye faint, and weary,
Howe'er your ailments vary,
Come hither, and make sure
Of a most perfect cure.

Here lies in death's embraces
My Bridegroom, Lord and God!
With awe my soul retraces
The dark and dolorous road,
That leads to this last station
Here in sweet meditation
I'll dwell by day and night,
Till faith is changed to sight.

This great musician, financier and bishop was also the author of that most popular Palm Sunday chant, "Blessed Is He That Comes," or "Hosanna in the Highest," and of the following doxologies:

O, form us all while we remain
On earth, unto Thy praise!

The Lord bless and keep thee in His favor
As His chosen property.

With Thy presence, Lord our Head and Saviour,
Bless us all we humbly pray!

The great Revival which began in 1727 continued for many years in ever increasing force and constantly widening influence. Eleven years later under the leadership of Peter Boehler the great Revival began in England. Among Boehler's many spiritual children was a young clergyman of the Church of England by name of John Gambold, an Oxford graduate and a particular friend of the Wesleys. He joined the Moravian Church and became its first English Bishop. Some of his hymns and sacred songs have become well known. One of his best is the Passion hymn greatly beloved in the Church of his choice:

> Go forth in spirit, go
> To Calvary's Holy Mount;
> See there thy Friend between two thieves,
> Suffering on thy account.

> Fall at His Cross's foot,
> And say: "My God and Lord,
> Here let me dwell and view those wounds
> Which life for me procured."

> His Blood thy cause will plead.
> Thy plaintive cry He'll hear,
> Look with an eye of pity down,
> And grant thee all thy prayer.

When the great English preacher, Rowland Hill, the friend and successor of Whitefield, had finished in his old age the last service of an arduous Sabbath day, he was observed walking up and down the church floor alone, repeating some verses. The aged preacher was quoting Bishop Gambold's hymn ending with the last two stanzas:

> And when I'm to die,
> Receive me, I'll cry,
> For Jesus hath loved me,
> I cannot tell why.

> But this I do find,
> We two are so joined,
> He'll not live in glory,
> And leave me behind.

Bishop Gambold's poem on the martyrdom of Ignatius, the friend of Polycarp, has become famous. Dr. Hanna, son-in-law and biographer of Dr. Thomas Chalmers, records that "no passage of English poetry was so frequently quoted by Dr. Chalmers in his latest years as the speech of Polycarp in this poem." Rev. Thomas Grinfield refers to this in his tribute to Bishop Gambold:

> Illustrious Chalmers, in his ample mind,
> The memory of Moravian Gambold shrined,
> Charmed with the deep tones of his tragic harp,
> And oft rehearsed those words of Polyearp.

Another of Peter Boehler's English converts was James Hutton, the famous book-seller. He, too, has given us some precious hymns such as the following:

> Teach me yet more of Thy blest ways,
> Thou slaughtered Lamb of God;
> And fix and root me in the grace,
> So dearly bought with blood.
> O tell me often of each wound,
> Of every grief and pain:
> And let my heart with joy confess
> From hence comes all my gain.

The best known English Moravian hymn-writer during the Great Revival is undoubtedly John Cennick, to whom reference was made in a previous chapter. His Bohemian ancestors, members of the Ancient Moravian Church, had found a refuge in England from cruel papal persecution. As soon as young Cennick heard of the renewal of the Church of his fathers, and became acquainted with its leaders, men like Zinzendorf, Spangenberg, Boehler and especially Gambold and Hutton, he at once felt himself at home and became the greatest preacher and evangelist the church has ever had. Count Zinzendorf called him "Paul Revived," and George Whitefield, his personal friend and fellow-worker, said of him:

"He was truly a great soul, one of those 'weak things,' which God hath chosen to confound the strong. Such a hardy worker with his hands and such a hearty preacher at the same time, I have scarce known. All call him a second Bunyan."

John Cennick has given us the story of his conversion in the well-known hymn:

Jesus, My All to Heaven is gone!

In the last two stanzas we find the sum and substance of his experience of salvation and joyful service:

> Lo, glad I come, and Thou, blest Lamb,
> Shalt take me to Thee as I am;
> My sinful self to Thee I give;
> Nothing but love shall I receive.
>
> Then will I tell to sinners round,
> What a dear Saviour 1 have found;
> I'll point to Thy redeeming Blood
> And say, 'Behold the way to God!'

His best known hymn, which is to be found in every church hymnal of English Protestantism is the one in which he sets forth his own poetic inspiration and purpose:

> Children of the Heavenly King,
> As ye journey sweetly sing;
> Sing your Saviour's worthy praise,
> Glorious in His works and ways.
>
> We are travelling home to God
> In the way the fathers trod;
> They are happy now, and we
> Soon their happiness shall see.
>
> Lift your eyes, ye sons of light,
> Zion's city is in sight;
> There our endless home shall be,
> There our Lord we soon shall see.

Questions for Chapter 5

QUESTION 1:

Chadwick's comment of owing "everything to the gift of Pentecost" should cause us to seek Him. How did Chadwick suggest it?

He said that he sought what he "knew not what. I knew that it was a bigger thing and a deeper need than I had ever known." Would you take a moment and seek this from the Lord, as did Samuel Chadwick?

QUESTION 2:

If you came from a Christian family, do you recall them singing and praising the Lord in their everyday life, regardless of whether it was easy or hard?

Do you live life with constant joy?

QUESTION 3:

How do you reconcile Ephesians 2:18 with the quote, "Seldom do we find a Moravian hymn or prayer in those days directed to the Father."

QUESTION 4:

Where "does the believer grow in true holiness?"

How?

And are you?

QUESTION 5:

Note the various people that wrote hymns. You may not be a hymn-writer, but do you record your thoughts of Him, back to Him?

Do you record these thoughts somewhere?

And then if you do, when was the last time you reviewed them?

If you journal, consider reviewing the previous week's notes on the weekend, and then the previous month's notes at the end of the month. And then carve out an entire weekend at the end of the year and reread your notes for the whole year. You will come away with your own song in your heart.

QUESTION 6:

Note the first stanza of Christian Frederick Gregor's hymn. Surely, you've found hidden treasure in Christ. Can you innumerate it?

Have you recently shared this treasure with another? Why or why not?

QUESTION 7:

Do you think Rowland Hill was scared to death of death when he quoted the lines referred to above?

QUESTION 8:

It is said of John Sennick that upon returning to the Moravian church and meeting acquainting himself with some of the leaders, that "he at once felt himself at home." Is there some locale or group where you "feel at home?"

Why or why not?

And what can you do about it?"

QUESTION 9:

The hymn which ends this chapter has this line, "Sing your Saviour's worthy praise." "Praise" is vastly different from thanking Him (which God loves to hear too).

If thanking the Lord is "me-centered," how would you describe praise?

QUESTION 10:

Why don't we focus more on the blood of Christ?

What do we focus on?

"I believe there is one thing for which God is very angry with our land, and for which His Holy Spirit is so little among us, viz., the neglect of united prayer, the appointed means of bringing down the Holy Spirit. I say it, because I believe it, that the Scotch with all their morality so-called, and their outward decency, respectability, and love of preaching, are not a praying people. Sirs, is not this the truth? The neglect of prayer proves to my mind, that there is a large amount of practical infidelity. If the people believed that there was a real, existing, personal God, they would ask Him for what they wanted, and they would get what they asked. But they do not ask, because they do not believe or expect to receive. Why do I say this? Because I want to get Christians to remember that though preaching is one of the great means appointed by God for the conversion of sinners, yet, unless God give the increase, Paul may plant and Apollos may water in vain; and God says He will be inquired of. O ministers, excuse me,-you gave me this chance of speaking-urge upon your people to come to the prayer-meeting. O Christians, go more to the prayer-meetings than you do. And when you go to the prayer-meeting, try and realize more that there is use in prayer."

— Evangelist Brownlow North to the Presbyterian General Assembly of Scotland.

"From the day of Pentecost, there has been not one great spiritual awakening in any land which has not begun in a union of prayer, though only among two or three; no such outward, upward movement has continued after such prayer meetings have declined; and it is in exact proportion to the maintenance of such joint and believing supplication and intercession that the Word of the Lord in any land or locality has had free course and been glorified."

— The late Arthur T. Pierson, D. D., Editor "The Missionary Review."

Chapter 6

FRUIT THAT ABIDES

A GREAT traveler of that period bore the following striking testimony: "In all my journeys I have found only three objects that exceeded my expectations, viz.: the ocean, Count Zinzendorf, and the Herrnhut congregation." However extravagant this praise may appear, there was certainly some reason for such enthusiastic eulogy. The great revival which began in 1727 had continued for more than a generation, constantly growing in extent and power. Herrnhut had become a spiritual city set on a hill that could not be hid. From all parts of Europe people had come hither either to be saved or to be baptized with the Holy Ghost and with fire. John Wesley's visit to Herrnhut may truly be called typical of thousands of others.

"God has given me at length," he wrote to his brother Samuel, "the desire of my heart. 1 am with a Church whose conversation is in Heaven; in whom is the mind that was in Christ, and who so walk as He walked." In his journal he wrote: "I would gladly have spent my life here; but my Master called me to labour in another part of His vineyard." "O when shall this Christianity cover the earth, as the waters cover the sea?" "Four times I enjoyed the blessing of hearing Christian David (a carpenter) preach. Thrice he described the state of those who are weak in faith; who are justified, but have not yet a new, clean heart; who have received forgiveness through the blood of Christ, but have not received the constant indwelling of the Holy Ghost." "This he yet again explained from the Scriptures which describe the state the Apostles were in from our Lord's death (and indeed for some time before) till the descent of the Holy Ghost on the day of Pentecost. They then had faith, otherwise He could not have prayed for them that 'their faith might not fail.' Yet they had not in the full sense 'new hearts'; neither had they received the gift of the Holy Ghost."

Who can fail to find in these lines of John Wesley the seed truths, if not the sum and substance, of those doctrines and experiences which became the mighty slogans of Methodism? Thus great revival waves continued to go out from Herrnhut, reaching ultimately to the uttermost parts of the earth. And now its great human leader, Count Zinzendorf, is about to be called home. To his family and friends the dying saint triumphantly said: "I am going to my Saviour. I am ready. There is nothing to hinder me now. I cannot say how much I love you all. Who would have believed that the prayer of Christ, 'that they all may be one,' could have been so strikingly fulfilled among us! I only asked for first-fruits among the heathen, and thousands have been given me. Are we not as in Heaven! Do we not live together like the angels! The Lord and His servants understand each other. I am ready."

A few hours later as his son-in-law pronounced the Old Testament benediction, "The Lord bless thee and keep thee, the Lord make His face shine upon thee and be gracious unto thee, the Lord lift up His countenance upon thee and give thee peace," this dear man of God fell asleep in Jesus and was absent from the body and at home with his Lord.

More than four thousand followed him to his resting place on the Hutberg, among them Moravian from Holland, England, Ireland, North America and Greenland. On his tombstone the following inscription was placed:

"Here lie the remains of that immortal man of God, Nicholas Lewis, Count and Lord of Zinzendorf and Pattendorf; who through the grace of God and his own unwearied service, became the ordinary of the Brethren's Church, renewed in this eighteenth century. He was born in Dresden on May 26th, 1700, and entered into the joy of His Lord at Herrnhut on May 9th, 1760. He was appointed to bring forth fruit, and that his fruit should abide."

Bishop Evelyn Hasse has called attention to the following fruit to be found on the Moravian tree in the garden of the Lord:

"It was the Herald Church of the greatest European Revival ever known, having been a Reformed Church sixty years before the Reformation.

"It was one of the sources of the Evangelical Revival here in England, and no small factor in its spread.

"It led the way in the Missionary Revival, having as a Church, been engaged in evangelizing the heathen more than half a century before the rest of Protestantism.

"In the Educational Movement it did pioneer work, both from the religious side and also as a part of the Revival of learning.

"It published the first Protestant Hymn Book in Europe, both in Bohemian and German; it issued here in England in 1754 what Dr. Gregory in his Hymn Book of the Modern Church has described as the earliest great Catholic collection with which I am acquainted, which deserves a place beside Palgraves Treasury of Sacred Songs."

Particular attention is called to the abiding and abounding nature of two kinds of fruit above enumerated, viz.: Foreign Missions and Sacred Songs. Through its Foreign Missions the Moravian Church is best known and most beloved. Testimonials abound not only from the great Protestant Churches and Missionary Societies, but also from modern explorers and travelers such as Swen Hedin, the Roosevelts and Leut. MacMillan. Theodore Parker once said that if the Foreign Missionary movement had done nothing more than to produce such a character as Adoniram Judson, it were well worth all its cost.

The same may be affirmed of many Moravian Missionaries. Their lives and unselfish services are the glory of Christ and the Church. David Zeisberger and his sixty years of self-sacrificing labors among the American Indians is fruit which abides today. Frederich Martin, one of the first Moravian Missionaries to the Negroes on the island of St. Thomas, was one of the Lord's chosen vessels and a typical Moravian. He and a fellow worker were put in jail chiefly for preaching the Gospel to the Blacks. More than three months were spent in a miserable prison; but the Spirit filled missionaries gave themselves to prayer like Paul and Silas in the Philippian dungeon. Their faithful Negro congregation, nearly 700 communicants, gather daily as near the jail as possible to join in singing and hear the sermons of their captive ministers. A great revival follows and large numbers are converted. Suddenly Count Zinzendorf arrives on his first Missionary journey, accompanied by two couples to reinforce the over-worked and imprisoned missionaries. As the ship draws near the beautiful island the Count said to his fellow workers:

"What if we find no one here? What if the missionaries are all dead?" To this one of the young workers quietly replied: "Then we are here," whereupon Count Zinzindorf uttered the oft quoted exclamation, "Gens aeterna, these Maehren!" "An eternal race, these Moravians!" The Count soon secured the freedom from jail of the sick and half-starved missionaries. He was amazed at the greatness of Frederich Martin's work and wrote back to Germany: "St. Thomas is a much more wonderful miracle than our own Herrnhut." After fourteen years of most sacrificial service Frederich Martin has reached the end of his earthly pilgrimage. More than fifty of his fellow workers have already laid down their lives. To his weeping wife the dying missionary says: "My dear heart, 1 shall probably soon go to my Saviour. Do thou always be happy in Him. With me it is unspeakably well, and if my spirit flies away to Him, please ask the Governor to permit my earthly tabernacle to rest on the plantation beside our Chapel."

When his death was announced to the congregation the place became such a scene of weeping that the service had to be brought to a sudden close. Of such trials and triumphs of faith the history of Moravian Foreign Missions is full to overflowing and they constitute our richest heritage and our most glorious and abiding fruitage. "They overcame by the blood of the Lamb, and by the word of their testimony, and they loved not their lives even unto death." (Rev. 12:11.)

The other great and most abiding contribution of the Moravian Church is its Hymnology. In proportion to its size it has given far more hymns to Christendom than any other Protestant denomination. This precious offering of sacred song may be traced directly to the Great Revival. In a former chapter this has already been demonstrated. The following illustrations will more fully confirm this claim.

The great Moravian poet-preacher and evangelist, John Cennick, is conducting one of his famous open air meetings. Multitudes flock to hear him and are born again through faith in the precious blood. One day a young Scotch day-laborer by name of John Montgomery is awakened and converted through the preaching of Cennick. He joins the Moravian Church and thus John and Mary Montgomery become Moravian missionaries. On a little island in the West Indies lie their earthly remains waiting for "the shout, the voice of the Archangel and the trumpet of God." Their little son James is educated in the Moravian school at Fulneck and becomes ultimately the greatest writer of hymns the Church has ever produced.

In many of the large Protestant hymn books, the following authors are generally found in the first rank: Isaac Watts, Charles Wesley and James Montgomery. The latter has certainly written some of the finest hymns in the English language. The following first lines will indicate how wide and varied their scope as well as how rich and spiritual their substance:

Angels, from the realms of glory
Wing your flight o'er all the earth;

Hail to the Lord's anointed,
Great David's greater Son;

Go to dark Gethsemane,
Ye that feel the tempter's power;

In the hour of trial,
Jesus, plead for me;

Hark the song of jubilee,
Loud as mighty thunders roar;

The Lord is my Shepherd, no want shall I know;
1 feed in green pastures, safe-folded I rest;

Sing we the song of those who stand
Around the eternal Throne;

Servant of God, well done!
Rest from thy loved employ;

Prayer is the soul's sincere desire,
Uttered or unexpressed;

Sow in the morn thy seed,
At eve hold not thy hand;

Come to Calvary's holy mountain
Sinners, ruined by the fall;

Jesus, our best beloved Friend,
Draw out our souls in pure desire;
Jesus, in love to us descend,
Baptize us with Thy Spirit's fire.

For ever with the Lord!
Amen, so let it be!
Life from the dead is in that word,
'Tis immortality.

At a great missionary meeting in Liverpool over which the famous
Methodist preacher and scholar, Dr. Adam Clarke presided, James
Montgomery was one of the speakers. The beloved poet often referred
to his dear parents who laid down their lives for Christ in a foreign field
and exclaimed: "They finished well. 1, too, am the son of a
missionary." He closed his address on this occasion by reciting a
missionary hymn which he had just composed, viz., the one beginning:

Hail to the Lord's Anointed.

Dr. Adam Clarke was so impressed by its spiritual depth and beauty
that he requested the author's permission to publish it in his now
famous Commentary. Thus James Montgomery's seven stanzas occupy
nearly a full page in this great work in connection with the seventy-
second Psalm, of which it is a partial paraphrase. Dr. Clarke introduced
it with this note:

"The following poetical version of some of the principal passages of
the foregoing Psalm was made and kindly given me by my much
respected friend, James Montgomery, Esq., of Sheffield. I need not tell
the intelligent reader that he has seized the spirit and exhibited some of
the principal beauties of the Hebrew bard; though, (to use his own
words in his letter to me) his 'hand trembled to touch the harp of Zion.'
1 take the liberty here to register a wish which I have strongly expressed
to himself, that he would favor the Church of God with a metrical
version of the whole Book."

One more instance may be given of the abiding fruit of this great revival
both as it relates to foreign missions and the songs of Zion. About the
same time as the preceding incident took place, Dr. Thomas Chalmers
was on his way to London to preach the annual Missionary sermon for
one of the great societies-a sermon which gave him a world-wide
reputation as a Christian thinker and orator. On his way to this
appointment he turns aside to Sheffield in order to become personally
acquainted with James Montgomery and gather additional facts and
inspiration for his great arguments. This visit was described years after

in a letter from Montgomery to Dr. William Hanna and is found in his excellent biography of Dr. Chalmers. It is in part as follows:

"On a dark night in April (I have forgotten the year) two strangers called at my house in Sheffield; one of whom introduced himself as Mr. Smith, bookseller of Glasgow, and his companion as the Rev. Dr. Chalmers of the same city. Of course, I was glad to become personally acquainted with so great and good a man, and we soon were earnestly engaged in conversation on subjects endeared to us both. Though at first I found it difficult to take in and decipher his peculiar utterance, yet the thoughts that spoke themselves through the seemingly uncouth words, came so quick and thick upon me from his lips, that I could not help understanding them; till being myself aroused into unwonted volubility of speech, I responded as promptly as they were made to his numerous and searching inquiries concerning the Moravians, among whom I was born, but especially respecting their scriptural method of evangelizing and civilizing barbarian tribes. In the outset he told me that he had come directly from Fulneck, one of our principal establishments in England, and where there is an academy for the education of children, in which I had been myself a pupil about ten years in the last century. At the time there were many scholars from the North, as well as Irish and English boarders, there. My visitor said that he had invited all the Scotch lads to meet him at the inn, and 'how many think you, there were of them?' he asked me. 'Indeed, I cannot tell,' I replied. He answered: 'There were saxtain or saventain.' (I cannot pretend to spell the numbers as he pronounced them to my unpracticed ear) and I was so taken by surprise that I exclaimed abruptly: 'It is enough to corrupt the English language in the Seminary.' In that moment I felt I had uttered an impertinence, though without the slightest consciousness of such an application to my hearer. Instantly recovering my presence of mind I added: 'When I was at Fulneck school, I was the only Scotch lad there.' An angel visit short and bright it was to me, and I do not remember that I ever spent an hour of more animated and delightful intercommunion with a kindred spirit in my life. Our discourse turned principally on the subject of Moravian Missions in pagan lands, and the inability of our few and small congregations to raise among themselves the pecuniary expenses of maintaining their numerous establishments in Greenland, Labrador, North and South America, the West Indies and South Africa. Hereupon

Dr. Chalmers exclaimed: 'I mean to raise five hundred pounds for the Brethren's Missions this year.' 'Five hundred pounds for our poor Missions,' I cried; 'I never heard of such a thing before.' He rejoined, 'I will do it.' But while I heartily thanked him, and implicitly believed in the integrity of his intentions, I could only hope he might be able to fulfill it, and within myself I said, 'I will watch you, doctor.' I did so, and traced him through sermons, subscriptions, collections and donations, till these had realized a sum nearer six than five hundred pounds."

How better can we close this chapter on the abiding fruit of the Great Revival as it is to be found chiefly in Moravian Missions and in Moravian Hymns than with the touching Missionary prayer of James Montgomery, himself the indirect product of this mighty movement;

O Spirit of the living God,
In all Thy plenitude of grace,
Where'er the foot of man hath trod,
Descend on our apostate race.

Give tongues of fire and hearts of love
To preach the reconciling word;
Give power and unction from above,
Where'er the joyful sound is heard.

O Spirit of the Lord, prepare
All the round earth her God to meet'
Breathe Thou abroad like morning air,
Till hearts of stone begin to beat.

Baptize the nations; far and nigh
The triumphs of the Cross record;
The name of Jesus glorify,
Till every kindred call Him Lord!

Questions for Chapter 6

QUESTION 1:

Note John Wesley's comments on the conversations of the Moravians. The friends that you hang out with, where is their conversation?

QUESTION 2:

Note Evangelist Brownlow North's strong rebuke of his own people. Can the same be said of you?

Are you hoping in vain for conversions of people around you?

QUESTION 3:

If the carpenter preacher were giving the alter call in your church and he went over the lost-ness of folks for the third time, would you be looking at your watch?

QUESTION 4:

Note the paragraph where Zinzendorf is talking about going home to heaven. He says, "Are we not as in Heaven!" He is partially quoting scripture. What scripture is he quoting?

And how did he apply it to the lives of the Moravian church members?

QUESTION 5:

What are the two kinds of fruit that are both "abiding and abounding" from the Moravian church?

_____   _____

and

_____   _____

QUESTION 6:

Have you ever been on a mission trip?

How did it impact you?

QUESTION 7:

Reading James Montgomery's "first-lines" of his hymns, do you notice that they are all scripture verses rewritten?

Can you identify which verses they are?

And then, can you see how you can pray those "first-lines" to the Lord as prayers?

Practice praying with a few of those lines.

QUESTION 8:

James Montgomery said that, "his hand trembled to touch the harp of Zion." What did he mean by that?

Does your hand tremble in the same way when you come to Scripture?

Why or why not?

QUESTION 9:

Giving financially to missions is noted above. Do you give regularly to missions?

To whom do you give, and why?

Are you doing this above and beyond your tithing?

Why or why not?

QUESTION 10:

In the last line of the last stanza of the last prayer/hymn of this chapter, James Montgomery tells us how to pray for the lost. Do you know the scripture/s that he references in this last line?

Does this challenge how you pray for the lost?
How does it challenge you, if it does?

"Standing in the foreground of all Paul's mental processes was Jesus the Messiah. From the moment of his conviction that Jesus was the Messiah he transferred everything in Judaism to the head of Christ, and at once we had the doctrine and science of Christology in its highest development. Paul did not bother much about the direct words attributed to Jesus. Few of these are mentioned in his epistles. They were jewels, it is true; but he had a still greater jewel; and this was the Death of Jesus on the Cross. This was for Paul the center of all things, the event which made forgiveness of sin possible, and which was demanded by the justice of God. It was by Jesus' death that Paul himself had conquered death and had obtained forgiveness and life."

— *The Christian World*, Professor Adolph Harnack of Berlin

—

"Scotland, happily, is still very rich in great preachers, scholars and theologians, but I think they will be the foremost to admit that none of them is quite on the same level as the master we mourn-Principal James Denney.... His wife, who gave him the truest and most perfect companionship, led him into a more pronounced evangelical creed. It was she who induced him to read Spurgeon, whom he had been inclined to despise. He became an ardent admirer of the preacher and a very careful and sympathetic student of his sermons. It was Spurgeon perhaps as much as any one who led him to the great decision of his life, the decision to preach the Atoning Death of the Lord Jesus Christ. This was all in all to him. He spent and was spent in making it everything to the Church."

— Sir W. Robertson Nicholl's appreciation of Principal
James Denney author of "The Death of Christ."

Chapter 7

RENEW OUR DAYS

TURN Thou us unto Thee, O Lord, and we shall be turned; renew our days as of old. (Lamentations 5:21). This was the closing prayer of Israel's great prophet Jeremiah. This also was the dying petition of the great Bishop of the ancient Moravian Church, John Amos Comenius. And as young Count Zinzendorf read these words he exclaimed:

"I could not peruse the lamentations of old Comenius addressed to the Anglican Church-lamentations, called forth by the idea that the Church of the Brethren was coming to an end, and that he was locking its door, I could not read his mournful prayer, 'Turn Thou us unto Thee, O Lord, and we shall be turned; renew our days as of old,' without resolving there and then: 'I will, as far as I can, help to bring about this renewal. And though I have to sacrifice my earthly possessions, my honours and my life, as long as I live, and as far as I shall be able to provide even after my death, I will do my utmost that this little company of the Lord's disciples shall be preserved for Him, until He comes.'"

We do well to register a similar vow and holy resolve, This great celebration of our Spiritual Renewal as a Church two hundred years ago will stir every true Moravian to pray, "Renew our days as of old."

In the beautiful and inspiring "Memorial" so graciously presented to us by the chief officials of the Federal Council of the Churches of Christ in America, we find these earnest closing words:

"Praying for your Historic Church a renewal of those spiritual experiences which gave you so much power two hundred years ago, let us express to you in the name of the Churches the great sense of obligation we feel for your spiritual leadership."

This last chapter may well be devoted to a consideration of this concluding prayer, viz.: "Praying for your Historic Church a renewal of those spiritual experiences which gave you so much power two hundred years ago."

Two questions at once suggest themselves:

1. WHAT WERE THOSE EXPERIENCES?

2. HOW MAY THEY BE RENEWED?

Their first great experience which gave our fathers such spiritual power was

I. A Personal Experience of Salvation

They had found to their sorrow that there was no salvation from sin in good works or in Church and creeds, still less in their own faulty conduct, culture or character. They fled for refuge to Jesus the Crucified and, gazing upon the bleeding, dying, Lamb of God, they experienced a blessed sense of pardon and peace. Here it was that the Holy Spirit bore witness with their spirits that they had become by faith the children of God, having passed from death unto life.

This personal experience of salvation, this assurance of their pardon and adoption into the family of God, gave our fathers such boldness and power in testimony not only in heathen lands, but also in the chief cities of the world, in the universities and royal courts of Europe.

Personal experience of salvation was described by Count Zinzendorf in one of their first Synods in the following sentences:

1. Justification is the forgiveness of sins.
2. The moment a man flies to Christ he is justified.
3. And has peace with God, but not always joy.
4. Nor, perhaps, may he know he is justified till long after.
5. For the assurance of it is distinct from justification itself.
6. But others may know he is justified by his power over sin, by his seriousness, his love of the brethren, and his hunger and thirst after righteousness, which alone prove the spiritual life to be begun.
7. To be justified is the same thing as to be born of God.
8. When a man is awakened, he is begotten of God, and his fear and sorrow, and sense of the wrath of God, are the pangs of the new birth.

On a certain occasion when ordaining a missionary, Count Zinzendorf asked him, "Brother John, dost thou know His wounds? Hast thou sought and found pardon through their merit?"

In order that every member of the Church might have this personal experience of salvation each congregation was divided into the following five classes:

1. Those who are spiritually dead.
2. Those who are awakened and seek to be saved.
3. Babes in Christ, i. e., new converts.
4. Young men in Christ.
5. Fathers in Christ. I. John 2:12-13.

Another great leader in those wonderful days and years of revival was Peter Boehler. He defines this personal experience of salvation in the following six sentences:

1. When a man has living faith in Christ, then he is justified.
2. This is always given in a moment.
3. And in that moment he has peace with God.
4. Which he cannot have without ultimately knowing that he has it.
5. And, being born of God, he sinneth not.
6. Which deliverance from sin he cannot have without knowing that he has it."

Of Boehler's two distinguished converts, John and Charles Wesley, the latter through his matchless hymns, has wielded the greater influence. He has truly been called "The Prince of Christian Poets." But while he had the fire of poetic genius from birth, not a single Gospel hymn did he write until he had experienced the new birth.

The story of his conversion is most striking and instructive. Boehler's interview with him is thus described by Charles Wesley himself in his journal:

"At eleven I awakened in extreme pain, which I thought would quickly separate soul and body. Soon after Peter Boehler came to my bedside. I asked him to pray for me. He seemed unwilling at first, but beginning very faintly, he raised his voice by degrees, and prayed for my recovery with strange confidence. Then he took me by the hand and calmly said: 'You will not die now.' I thought within myself: 'I cannot hold out in this pain till morning. If it abates before, I believe I may recover.' He asked me: 'Do you hope to be saved?' 'Yes.' 'For what reason do you hope it?' 'Because I have used my best endeavors to serve God.' He shook his head and said no more. I thought him very uncharitable, saying in my heart: 'What? Are not my endeavors a sufficient ground of hope? Would he rob me of my endeavors? I have nothing else to trust to.'"

A few weeks later Wesley thus refers to another of the many visits of Peter Boehler.

"No sooner was l got to James Hutton's, having removed my things thither from his father's, than the pain in my side returned, and with that the fever. Having disappointed God in His last visitation, He has now again brought me to the bed of sickness. Towards midnight I received some relief by bleeding. In the morning Dr. Cockburn came to see me; and a better physician, Peter Boehler, whom God had detained in England for my good. He stood by my bedside, and prayed over me, that now at least I might see the divine intention in this and my late illness. I immediately thought it might be I should again consider Boehler's doctrine of faith; examine myself whether I was in the faith; and if I was not, never cease seeking and longing after it till I attained it."

To ask an apparently dying minister and a missionary at that, if he is saved, might almost seem an act of presumption and impertinence. But Christendom today may well thank God for this faithful Moravian who dared to probe the soul of Charles Wesley. For, as Dr. Charles Nutter, a well-known Methodist hymnologist, recently wrote in The Methodist Review:

"More than six thousand of Charles Wesley's hymns have been published. Wesley wrote verses from the time of his conversion in 1738 until the time of his last sickness in 1788, fifty years; but six thousand hymns would be one hundred and twenty a year, ten a month, or one hymn every three days for fifty years."

The majority of his hymns testify to his great experience of salvation. Peter Boehler had told him: "If I had a thousand tongues I would praise Jesus with every one of them." This prompted Wesley shortly after his conversion to write the immortal lines:

O for a thousand tongues to sing
My dear Redeemer's praise;
The glories of my God and King,
The triumphs of His grace.

He breaks the power of cancelled sin,
He sets the prisoner free;
His blood can make the foulest clean,
His blood availed for me.

The question has been asked whether this amazing experience made by Charles Wesley may truly be called his conversion. He himself so regarded it. The change it worked in him was indeed radical. Old things passed away; all things became new. This experience of salvation caused him, who according to his own testimony was building his hopes of Heaven on his own endeavors and had nothing else to trust to, to cry out in anguish of soul,

Depth of mercy, can there be
Mercy still reserved for me,
Can my God His wrath forbear,
Me, the chief of sinners spare?

I have long withstood His grace,
Long provoked Him to His face,
Would not hearken to His calls,
Grieved Him by a thousand falls.

Having found pardon and peace at the Cross, Wesley soon discovered that he can enjoy this experience of salvation only as he continues to abide in the Crucified One. Hence he utters the touching prayer:

For ever here my rest shall be,
Close to Thy pierced side;
This all my hope and all my plea,
For me the Saviour died.

My dying Saviour and my God,
Fountain for guilt and sin,
Sprinkle me ever with Thy blood,
And cleanse and keep me clean.

A number of years after his conversion Wesley wrote another great hymn on the atonement, "Arise, My Soul, Arise!" Its theology, as well as its language, still bear witness to the power of that great experience of salvation into which under God, Boehler had led him. The third and fourth stanzas are distinctly Moravian in their teaching and phraseology:

> Five bleeding wounds He bears,
> Received on Calvary;
> They pour effectual prayers,
> They strongly plead for me:
> "Forgive him, oh forgive," they cry,
> "Nor let that ransomed sinner die."

> The Father hears Him pray,
> His dear anointed one.
> He cannot turn away,
> The presence of His Son;
> The Spirit answers to the blood,
> And tells me I am born of God.

The second great experience which gave our fathers such spiritual power and leadership was

II. The Baptism with the Holy Ghost.

On this point we wish to quote the words of one of our own beloved pastors, Dr. J. Kenneth Pfohl. In a recent article in The Moravian he wrote: "The great Moravian Pentecost was not a shower of blessing out of a cloudless sky. It did come suddenly, as suddenly as the blessing of its greater predecessor in Jerusalem, when the Christian Church was born. Yet, for long, there had been signs of abundance of rain, though many recognized them not. In short, the blessing of the thirteenth of August, 1727, was diligently and earnestly prepared for. We know of no annals of Church history which evidence greater desire for an outpouring of the Holy Spirit and more patient and persistent effort in that direction than those of our own church between the years 1725 and 1727. Two distinct lines of preparation and spiritual effort for the blessing are evident. One was prayer; the other was 'individual work with individuals.' We are told that 'men and women met for prayer and praise at one another's homes and the Church of Bertheisdorf was crowded out.' Then the Spirit came in great power. Then the entire company experienced the blessing at one and the same time."

This baptism with the Holy Spirit endued our fathers with power from. on high. They experienced exactly what has been so eloquently described by that prince of preachers, Dr. Alexander MacLaren, in his sermons on Ephesians:

"That power is given to us through the gift of the Divine Spirit. The very name of that Spirit is 'the Spirit of Might.' Christ spoke to us about being 'endued with power from on high.' The last of His promises that dropped from His lips upon earth was the promise that His followers should receive the power of the Spirit coming upon them. Wheresoever in the early histories we read of a man who was full of the Holy Ghost, we read that he was 'full of power.' It is power for service. 'Tarry ye in Jerusalem till ye be endued with power from on high.' There is no such force for the spreading of Christ's Kingdom and the witness-bearing work of His Church, as the possession of this Divine Spirit. Plunged into that fiery baptism, the selfishness and the sloth which stand in the way of so many of us, are all consumed and annihilated, and we are set free for service because the bonds that bound us are burnt up in the merciful furnace of His fiery power. 'Ye shall be strengthened with might by His Spirit in the inner man'-a power that will fill and flood all your nature, if you will let it, and make you strong to suffer, strong to combat, strong to serve, and to witness for your Lord."

Our Moravian Brethren knew this power two hundred years ago. They had experienced to a remarkable degree Pentecost. It is therefore not to be wondered at that our friends of the Federal Council are praying for our Church a "renewal of those spiritual experiences which gave us so much power two hundred years ago.

The writer of these lines was at one time pastor of the historic Moravian congregation at Nazareth, Pa. One of the first ministers of this charge, Francis C. Lembke, whose pastorate here extended from 1754 to 1784, during which time he also founded the celebrated school now known as Nazareth Hall, is a remarkable illustration of the power of Calvary and of Pentecost as experienced in the Great Revival.

In 1733 this young man was a student at the University of Jena, working for a doctor's degree in philosophy. Some converted professors and students invited him to their prayer-meetings and the historian tells us the result:

"Through their efforts Lembke began to seek Christ with many prayers and tears. One evening, while praying, he realized, through the Holy Spirit, that the blood of Jesus Christ had cleansed him from all sin, and rose from his knees accepted in the Beloved."

In course of time he is appointed to a professorship in Strasbourg and assistant Preacher in the Church of St. Peter. Of his great experience there we read:

"The more he prepared his sermons, the less warmth and life they had. Of this he was himself keenly conscious. His congregations decreased every Sunday until at last he preached almost to empty benches. He felt that he was not fitted for the pulpit, and on one occasion became so utterly discouraged while preparing, that he secured a substitute for the next day, late on Saturday night. He now made his preaching the subject of special prayer, beseeching the Lord, either to relieve him of this duty, or to loose his tongue and give him grace to proclaim the Gospel. The wonderful answer to these prayers we will set forth in Lembke's own words: 'One day, when I entered the pulpit in great fear, crying for aid, the Lord suddenly spoke to me His omnipotent word "Ephphatha." Pentecostal power was given to me, and to the astonishment of my hearers as well as to my own, I proclaimed the free grace of God in Christ with an overflowing heart and with utmost freedom of speech.'

"From that day he preached sermons that caused a sensation throughout the city. The Church of St. Peter was crowded, whenever he appeared in the pulpit. In a little while the aisles, and even the pulpit steps were filled with hearers, until the building could not contain the multitude which flocked together."

Let it be carefully noted that this mighty baptism with the Holy Ghost was received in answer to earnest and importunate prayer. It is strictest truth what our brethren of the Federal Council in their Memorial declare: "Your great historic revival began in prayer. Therefore the Holy Spirit was mightily poured out among you." It is perfectly Scriptural and in fullest harmony with the history of every great revival that believers meet together to pray for the Holy Spirit. God still pours water on those who are thirsty and His Spirit upon them that ask Him. Taking time to pray and to wait upon the Lord, as our fathers did, will insure us a "renewal of those spiritual experiences which gave them so much power two hundred years ago."

The nearest approach to that great revival two hundred years ago is the recent outpouring of the Holy Spirit in Korea. How did that wonderful movement begin, which some one has called "an appendix to the Book of Acts." The historian of the revival tells us:

"A few missionaries decided to meet together to pray daily at noon. At the end of the month one brother proposed that 'as nothing had happened, the prayer meeting should be discontinued. Let us each pray at home as we find it convenient,' said he. The others, however, protested that they ought rather to spend even more time in prayer each day. So they continued the daily prayer-meeting for four months.

Then suddenly the blessing began to be poured out. Church services here and there were broken up by weeping and confessing of sins. At length a mighty revival broke out. And when the Church was purified, many sinners found salvation. Multitudes flocked to the churches. Some came to mock, but fear laid hold of them, and they stayed to pray.

"One of the missionaries declared: 'It paid well to have spent several months in prayer; for when God gave the Holy Spirit, He accomplished more in half a day than all the missionaries together could have accomplished in half a year. In less than two months more than 2,000 heathen were converted. The burning zeal of those converts has become a byword. Some of them gave all they had to build a church, and wept because they could not give more. Needless to say, they realized the power of prayer. These converts were themselves baptized with the "Spirit of supplication." In one church it was announced that a daily prayer-meeting would be held at 4:30 every morning. The first day 400 people arrived long before the stated hour-eager to pray. The number rapidly increased to 600 as days went on. At Seoul 1100 is the average attendance at the weekly prayer-meeting.'"

"Verily the day of revivals is not past. The Holy Spirit is still waiting to fill believers with power from on high. The Lord is waiting to be gracious, and "they that wait upon the Lord shall renew their strength:

they shall mount up with wings as eagles; they shall run, and not be weary; they shall walk and not faint." (Is. 40:31.) Our brethren of the Federal Council utter the fervent prayer "that the glorious event which so mightily moved through you the religious life of the eighteenth century may have its duplication in the twentieth." God knows it is as sorely needed now as it was then. The two times are very much alike. Dead orthodoxy had degenerated into rationalism, worldliness, vice, crime and atheism. Then the great revival came and, as the historian Green tells us, saved England from plunging over the precipice into the unspeakable horrors of the French revolution. If civilization today is to be saved and become Christian, another revival is absolutely necessary. In a recent article in The Moravian, the President of our Provincial Elders Conference, Dr. E. S. Hagen, wrote as follows:

"The great revival in 1727 in Herrnhut was the normal and logical result of prayer and the preaching of the Word of the Cross. "Christ and Him Crucified" was our Brethren's Confession of Faith, and the inward witness of remission of sins through faith in His blood," their blessed and quickening experience. Lecky in his "History of Morals," says of John Wesley's conversion May 24, 1738, in the prayer meeting of Moravian Brethren in Aldersgate street: "What happened in that little room was of more importance to England than all the victories of Pitt by land or sea." Our honored President, Calvin Coolidge, never said a truer thing than when he gave as his deliberate conviction that "What this country needs is a revival of religion." A renewal of our days as of old involves a return to fervent prayer and to the earnest and effectual preaching of the remission of sins through the vicarious sacrifice and the shedding of the blood of Jesus Christ, the Son of God. Revival time is coming. We cherish a high expectancy of it. Sooner than we dream of, to God's people, who give themselves to earnest, persevering prayer, and the Scriptural testimony concerning the Gospel of our Lord Jesus Christ, the windows of Heaven will be opened."

God grant the speedy fulfillment of our dear brother's wish and prayer! Let us ponder the remarkable testimony delivered several years ago at Northfield, Mass., by that beloved man of God, whose praise is in all the churches, Dr. F. B. Meyer:

"Those of you who visit London might very well walk down from Holborn to Fleet Street by a little street which is known as Fetter Lane.

When you are halfway down Fetter Lane, on your left hand you will see a very simple doorway, and over it the words, "Moravian Chapel." Whenever I go down that street I stop there for a moment and lift my hat. I feel as I felt by Moody's grave this morning.

"What happened there? Well, Wesley, as you know, came to America, to Savannah, but he did not accomplish anything very great, for he had not yet reached the dynamic of which I am talking. He was an ordinary man. He came back to London, and in London he met a very remarkable man, Peter Boehler. Peter Boehler was connected with Count Zinzendorf. The Moravians are the disciples of John Huss, as you know, and they lived in the power of the Holy Spirit of which I am now talking. Wesley learned all he knew from those godly people.

"When he came back again to Aldersgate Street he met forty or fifty people and asked them to meet him again at five o'clock that afternoon in the Fetter Lane chapel; and they did. Wesley, his brother, Whitefield, and a number more whose names are written in the book of life were there. They remained for some time quiet, searching their hearts. Then they waited on God, and in the fellowship of that hour they became conscious of the movement of the Spirit of God. They fell on their faces, Wesley says in his journal, and lay there, overcome with gratitude, and then they rose and sang the 'Te Deum.'

"The next day Whitefield took the coach down to Bristol, and began preaching there in the power of the Holy Ghost. After about a month Wesley followed, and for forty years they went up and down our country in the face of every sort of resistance. If you read Wesley's sermons you will find them interesting, but neither the sermons of Whitefield nor Wesley have any traits of supreme genius. But they had the dynamic, they had the power of the Holy Spirit."

Our calling as a Moravian Church has been truly set forth by our great leader, Count Zinzendorf, in the following weighty sentence:

"I am destined by the Lord to proclaim the message of the death and blood of Jesus, not with human wisdom, but with divine power, unmindful of personal consequences to myself."

What is this declaration but the "Blood and Fire" slogan of the Salvation Army? It was the favorite phrase of Evan Roberts, the youthful leader of the Welsh Revival: "Remember the Blood! Catch the Flame."

We take our leave of these memorable events and persons with a parting look at that noble youth, fresh from the highest schools of learning, abounding in life, genius, and wealth, standing before the picture of the bleeding, dying Saviour, pondering the searching question, "This have I done for thee! What doest thou for me?" We hear him exclaim as his life's rule and motto:

I have one passion, it is Jesus, Jesus only.

We will heed his exhortation as he sings:

> Rise, go forth to meet the Lamb,
> Slumber not midst worldly care;
> Let your lamps be all on flame,
> For His Coming now prepare.
> Then whene'er you hear the cry,
> "Lo the Bridegroom draweth nigh,"
> You will not confounded be,
> But can meet Him joyfully.
>
> Let us walk the narrow way,
> Watchful, cheerful, free from toil;
> Trim our lamps from day to day,
> Adding still recruits of oil;
> Doubly doth the Spirit rest
> On his happy peaceful breast,
> Who himself to praying gives,
> Who a life of watching lives.

Questions for Chapter 7

QUESTION 1:

What is meant by the statement that "Paul's mental process [was to] transfer everything in Judaism to the head of Christ?"

QUESTION 2:

Think about your prayers, ". . . we shall be turned; renew our days as of old." When you pray thus, what are you praying for, your nation?

When Count Zinzendorf "sacrificed all," for what was he sacrificing?

QUESTION 3:

Take a moment and gaze "upon the bleeding, dying, Lamb of God." Has the "Holy Spirit borne witness with your spirit that you have become by faith a child of God, passed from death unto life. Have you experienced a blessed sense of pardon and peace?"

QUESTION 4:

What do you think Count Zinzendorf meant when he asked, "dost thou know His wounds?"

QUESTION 5:

Imagine asking a dying minister and missionary if he were saved? How does that challenge you, if it does?

And if it does not, why not?

QUESTION 6:

Wesley "discovered that he can enjoy this experience of salvation" even after the fact. How did he?

And how do you?

QUESTION 7:

When "a man who was full of the Holy Ghost [is] 'full of power' he accomplishes much. A couple of lines later we read what most Christians act like though, namely selfish and slothful. When are those "bonds that bind us burnt up?"

QUESTION 8:

In the words, "Taking time to pray and to wait upon the Lord, as our fathers did, will insure us a renewal" the writer is asking us to pray for revival to come, but there is something else that we see in their praying, and it is submission to the Lord. When you pray for the Lord to bring us renewal and revival, are you praying, submitting yourself to the Lord? Oh, that you would be doing that my friend.

QUESTION 9:

What is the difference in the Korean prayer meetings when compared to prayer meetings in your church?

QUESTION 10:

Amazing isn't it, that this quote is as appropriate for 1727, for 1927 and now, 2017?

Look again at this quote, "Dead orthodoxy had degenerated into rationalism, worldliness, vice, crime and atheism." Can you commit to praying as they, "TURN Thou us unto Thee, O Lord, and we shall be turned; renew our days as of old." (Lamentations 5:21)?

Learning Prayer Through the Fun of a Novel

Author Mark S Mirza works with churches, individuals and other ministries to help develop their prayer lives.

Troubles is the first book in **The Pray-ers** series. It is a fictional novel series where men and women model prayer in their daily lives. This book is a fun read as it dives into the power of prayer.

Troubles focuses on the lives of three prayer warriors, separated by hundreds of years and located on two different continents.

Read about the life and loves of Thales - Epaphrus' nephew from the the first century. Enjoy the Yankee turned southern itinerant preacher now living in Georgia and trying to minister after the War between the States (Alexander Rich) and the modern day track coach (Dr. Dale Riley) from Macon Poly Technic University.

Share their troubles, frustrations and triumphs as they talk with God through this avenue that we call Prayer.

They are **The Pray-ers** and they will give you hope and inspiration in your daily life.

And don't forget about the nine-foot tall angel or all of the demons... but you will need to read the book to find our more about them!

To order your copy of Volume one *Troubles* of **The Pray-ers** trilogy today, visit our website:

www.ThePray-ers.com

Or contact the author at:
Mark@CTMPrayer.org

Printed in Great Britain
by Amazon